Jeff has touched on a critical issue: the way our culture does *not* care for women. He has a plan for making a huge difference.

—JOHN ELDREDGE
Author of *Wild at Heart*

As a father of two daughters I am grateful that you are calling men to a higher standard and giving them hope and clarity in a world of despair and confusion.

—BANNING LIEBSCHER
Jesus Culture Founder and Pastor

Jeff details the stories of simple men who made valiant last stands on a moment's notice that will pierce your soul. The candor with which he shares his own struggles is both convicting and encouraging.

You don't need to have a wife or daughter to understand the importance of this message. If you have the X and Y chromosome, buy and read *Defending the Feminine Heart,* because a wall of properly constructed men defending the daughters of the King is what is needed now more than ever before in history.

—CLIFF GRAHAM
Author of the *Lion of War* Series

As the founder of a ministry that strengthens families and restores victims of sex-trafficking, I see every day the impact of a group of men who decide to let God love and lead them. I have witnessed men strengthen each other as they lock shields and go out to engage in good battle against the atrocities in this world.

These men find ways to protect their minds from being deceived by lies and do not allow their hearts to be trafficked by things that never fully satisfy. They are men who are standing strong, arms locked and ready for anything that comes against them, the women they love and those in their communities. And as a woman, that makes me feel more safe in this world.

I'm excited for you to read this book and be a part of this community. You will get what you need and be equipped to go out and be who you're meant to be.

Stand up and take your place in the wall. We need you.

—KATHRINE LEE
Founder, Pure Hope Foundation

This book is a must read for men. Pastor Jeff Voth does a masterful job of opening the eyes of men everywhere to realize their responsibility to become a wall of protection for their wives and daughters. I think he may have given Adam a bit of a bad rap, but Adam was definitely not a wall of protection for Eve! I like his emphasis on Jesus's special treatment of women in the New Testament. His analysis of the current paucity of manhood is piercingly true. And any pastor who needs great material for premarital counsel need look no further. He's got a list of questions to ask at the back of the book. I love the book. You need to read it.

—TERRY LAW
World Compassion Ministries

In true Jeff Voth fashion, there are no punches pulled in *Defending the Feminine Heart*. Jeff has truly identified the issue in our culture pertaining to the lack of biblical manhood and the problems involved when there is no moral compass.

In an age where chivalry has seemed to have lost its edge and objectifying women is the norm, Jeff brings us back to the basics of biblical manhood and calls men to be different— to be men who will stand up for God's daughters and walk counter culturally!

Identification of issues is one thing, but Jeff gives us the solution. *Defending the Feminine Heart* is a must read for any man or woman.

—JODY BURKEEN
Founder and Author of *Man Up God's Way*

Wow! *Defending the Feminine Heart* is not only a challenge, but also a wonderful encouragement! In this inspiring book, Jeff Voth invites men to join him on the journey to be real men—to protect the lives, hearts and reputations of the women around us. He has written a book that he illustrates with his own life! I've had the privilege of watching Jeff be a "wall" for his family…especially his wife and daughter! But Jeff has made a habit of being a wall for all those around him—the people he pastors, the students in the classes he teaches at a local university, and his friends!

Jeff writes with the toughness, yet tenderness, that he lives! *Defending the Feminine Heart* challenges readers with intensity and passion to lay down our lives in a way that is gentle and humble like our Master who Jeff continues to point us toward and seeks to follow in his own life. May we absorb the words of this book and may we become real men who are truly defending the feminine heart!

—KEITH WHEELER
Keith Wheeler Ministries

In *Defending the Feminine Heart*, Jeff Voth lays it on the line. He unashamedly calls out all men. He does so by challenging them to examine their hearts and their minds as it relates to how they treat all women, because, as he says in the book, "They are all His daughters (God's daughters)." Using Jesus as the supreme example, Jeff's book strategically and powerfully gives men a structure and a plan to regain our godly masculine design that has been perverted by our culture. He also includes examples of men who have stood for women in a heroic fashion, encouraging all of us to get off the sidelines and back into the battle, therefore living out the design God had for us from the very beginning, and with a servant/warrior's heart.

—THE HONORABLE TIM HARRIS
Former Tulsa County District Attorney (1999–2014)

This book is a clarion call for all men! This Holy Spirit led book is a must read for all men who wonder what it means to truly admire, love, and cherish women for the true gift from God they are. Jeff Voth has nailed it!

—JASON WEIS
Co-founder/President of The Demand Project

Defending the Feminine Heart is a powerful and practical approach to the godly call that Jesus has for every man. I am the father of three daughters, and I gleaned valuable insights that I could immediately put into practice in my home. If today's men will follow the precepts outlined in *Defending the Feminine Heart,* our homes, churches, and communities will thrive as a safe, flourishing, and impactful force for the glory of God!

—MICHAEL ALTSTIEL
Founder and Director
Know the Covering Ministries, Rapid City, SD

DEFENDING
the Feminine
HEART

DEFENDING
the Feminine
HEART

A Masculine Wall for **GOD'S** Daughters

BY JEFF VOTH

HONOR NET
PUBLISHERS
Sapulpa, OK

Defending the Feminine Heart
by Jeff Voth

ISBN 978-1-938021-45-9
Copyright © 2017 by Jeff Voth

Published by HonorNet
P. O. Box 910
Sapulpa, OK 74067

Printed in the United States of America
17 18 19 20 21 — 7 6 5 4 3 2 1

The Masculine Wall

After every chapter in Sections 1 and 2, there will be a short story about a man who has stood courageously as a wall for His daughters. I have no doubt that these stories will inspire you to follow the brave example these brothers have set.

From Lori

I'm honored to be able to share Lori's comments throughout the book in places where we felt the need for a feminine perspective. Throughout our marriage, I've been blessed by her unique viewpoint, and I've learned to rely on her wise insight. I know you'll be blessed by what she has to say.

Table of Contents

Section #1:
His Daughters

Section #2:
The Masculine Wall

Section #3:
Get Strategic

Prologue

I wrote this book because, in my opinion, we are failing miserably as a culture, largely due to the fact that we are raising weak men. To be more specific, I believe we are raising weak-minded men. Some of these men are predators. They are so weak minded that they have no power to resist the temptation to prey on women, young and old. They can't help but objectify women, both women they know and those they don't. And the sad truth is, many of the men who aren't predators, do nothing to stop those who are.

This is not the time to sit idly on the sidelines complaining about how bad things are getting. It's time to rise up! It's time for men to stand up and step in to their rightful place, their destined role.

What we need is a fire, a heavenly fire, kindled by the One who knows how to stir the hearts of men. We need a fire that rallies, a fire that burns, a blazing fire that burns up weakness and kindles greatness.

This book was written in the hope of igniting exactly that kind of fire in a few good men who are no longer content to sit on the bench. I am hoping, praying, and believing that, like the scattered embers of a campfire, those few men would come together and ignite a few more, spreading the fire, then igniting a few more, then spreading…igniting…spreading… igniting. I am standing as a wall of prayer, believing for this "ignition cycle" that will ultimately explode into an uncontrollable wildfire of good men. I'm praying for men who have been anointed and baptized by God's fire, men who will treat women as they deserve to be treated, like the precious gifts they are—daughters of the King…the King of kings.

It's no secret. There is a violent assault being waged in our culture today against our daughters—God's daughters. And if we don't learn to come together and stand as a wall of men, it will only get worse. This assault, this insidious attitude idolizes, objectifies, and then discards women. It uses and abuses, lures and manipulates. It's a sinister rhythm that began in the Garden between a serpent and a woman, a conversation witnessed by her man—a man who was supposed to be her wall…her protector.

This man was the one created to be her defense and her covering shield. But instead he just sat there while his woman, God's glorious gift, was deceived and then violated emotionally and spiritually. Our father, Adam, watched, hid, and then blamed his wife when asked about it later. He threw her under the bus while he hid behind her in the shrubs. Instead of a powerful wall of protection, he turned out to be a spineless wimp. And the really bad news is that this despicable trait has been passed on to every one of his sons, all the way down through the generations, all the way down to you and me.

Is there any hope?

Absolutely!

We can be changed. We can be honed into living stones, stones able to be fitted into a wall of manhood, made in the image of the Eternal Wall, the One who stands for us all.

My prayer is that as you read this book, He who hones stones will do His "wall making" work in you; so you will stop throwing women under the bus and get fired up to start standing as a wall of protection for them.

May the Lord help us all to stand as a wall for our wives and our daughters, because all of them are His daughters.

—JEFF VOTH
FROM THE CAVE, JULY 2016

∽ Section 1 ∾

His Daughters

This section is a description of my own journey as the father of a daughter. We'll take a close look at the way Jesus dealt with women and His treatment of them as His daughters. We'll compare that with the way today's Western culture treats women. The upper case H in the title of this section is capitalized for a reason. It's because every woman ever born on the planet is not just some guy's daughter. They are His; they are God's daughters. They are all His little girls, every one of them. This fact alone should set the tone for how we should treat all of the women in our lives. These precious women should be respected, honored, and cherished, not treated like objects to be used for our pleasure. Remember, at the end of days, we will all have to answer to their Daddy for the way we've treated His daughters.

Chapter 1

It's a Girl!

"I s it going to be a boy or a girl?"

That's usually the first question on the minds of couples when they find out they're pregnant. Today, with the advances in the medical community, couples don't have to wait until the baby is born to have an answer. That wasn't the case when Lori and I were waiting for our children to be born. More often than not, if we wanted to know the gender of the coming baby we had to rely on old wives' tales like the speed of the heart rate or how high or low the mother carried the baby. Older women would stand back, take a close look at Lori's belly, and confidently make their prediction.

I'll never forget the day our oldest son, Jacob, was born. I'd like to think I had no real preference whether my first child was a boy or a girl. But today, looking back, I'll have to admit…deep down I wanted a son. Whether it was the primal desire in the heart of every man to perpetuate the species or simply the desire to have a boy to carry on the Voth family name, I'm not sure. But the relationship with my own father is so special, so precious to me, I couldn't think of anything I wanted more than to have a son I could share my own life with.

I remember the moment when the doctor said, "It's a boy!" I shouted, "Yes!" My arms shot up in the "touchdown" pose, and I danced around the delivery room. For a moment I forgot all about Lori and the important role she'd played in the birth. In that grand moment, it was all about me and what I had done. I had produced a son! It wasn't until a few minutes later that I sheepishly realized…oh yeah, Lori had a little to do with this. Well, okay, Lori had a lot to do with this!

It was indeed a special moment. I swelled with pride as the thought sunk in. I had a son, and now there would be Voth men into the next generation and the world would be a safer place.

A little less than two years later Lori told me that she was pregnant again, and the familiar feelings of excitement and pride rushed back. For the next nine months my mind swirled with all those expectant thoughts. What would it be like to be the father of two boys? I dreamed of hunting and fishing, camping, and backpacking. We'd play sports and do all the manly stuff that men do together, my two boys and me.

Sure, it crossed my mind that the new baby could be a girl, but my mind didn't dwell on that very much because I really had no idea what I would do with a little girl. Playing house, dressing up dolls, and having tea parties wasn't in the top ten list of things that manly men did. So, yeah, I made up my mind that it would be best for our second child to be a boy, and I let the Lord know my decision (as if He needed input from me). I moved on to the important work of picking manly names, buying manly stuff, and making manly preparations.

On October 17, 1989, the powerful Loma Prieta earthquake rocked Northern California just before the first game of the World Series between the San Francisco Giants and the Oakland Athletics. But what I didn't know then was that, in just a few days, another earthquake was getting ready to rock my world.

The earthquake rumbled and caused horrific damage throughout Northern California. The game was postponed, but they kept the cameras on to cover the unfolding tragedy. The days that followed, I found myself glued to the television, focusing on the news of the earthquake and the many effects of it. However, on October 21, my mind had forgotten all about the earthquake in California. We were on our way to the hospital, and I was thinking about what our second son would look like. I couldn't wait to meet him face-to-face. What were we going to name him? I was lobbying hard for "Hank." "Hank Voth." Now there's a manly name!

It's a Girl!

We arrived at the hospital and were escorted to a delivery room. After a couple of hours of labor, the doctor came in to check on Lori and evaluate the progress of our baby's arrival. I'm no expert, but I had gone through this once before, and it was apparent to me that the time was close. I was excited. I was finally going to meet my second son!

There I was, looking the part of the expectant father, standing beside the bed with my green scrubs on. I couldn't wait to meet and hold Hank and introduce him to his big brother, Jacob. Like a catcher waiting for the first pitch, I was poised and ready. I heard the newborn cry. But the doctor's next words were like a punch in the gut. I reeled from the earth-quake rumbling through my head.

"Congratulations! It's a girl!"

"A what?"

"Jeff, you and Lori have a healthy baby girl!"

My ears heard his words, but my mind wasn't computing the content. I thought he just said that I had a baby girl. But that couldn't be right. He smiled as he gathered up the precious bundle and handed her over to me. After carefully checking the plumbing, I realized I hadn't misheard. The doctor was right. I was the father of a new baby girl!

I was stumped. How could I have missed it? How would this new devel-opment change my life? And what was this salty substance coming out of my eyes? Was there something in this piped-in hospital air that was causing my eyes to water? Of course not. I was crying, weeping like a… well, like a little girl. But I wasn't crying because I was sad or upset. My tears were like a heart-rain rolling down my cheeks coming from some-place deep within my masculine soul. My precious little Hannah Jeanne was only minutes old but she had the power to touch me in a profound way. Like a 7.0 earthquake, she shook me to my core. I knew from that moment on that I would never be the same.

As I held my newborn little girl I felt this overpowering need to protect her. I had only known her for a few minutes but she activated the father's heart within me, and I was overwhelmed by the desire to protect her from all enemies…especially boys! I felt myself being clothed with righteous armor. I was ready to take on all comers, to fight lions, giants, and teen-aged boys, regardless of their age or size.

In fact, when the nurse placed her in the nursery with the other newborns, I couldn't help but notice a little infant boy was just a little too close to her. I instructed the nurse that I would hold her personally responsible if he tried to reach over and touch her. She assured me that he was only an hour old, in his own incubator two feet away, and could not even see yet. But she would keep an eye on him just in case.

I could only shake my head. Wow. My first few moments with Jacob were awesome, but my first moments with Hannah Jeanne was an entirely new experience for me. This soft, sensitive, emotional, and beautiful little gift was opening my eyes and my heart in a brand-new way.

What a Knucklehead I Was

With every moment that went by, Hannah's new presence in our family was opening my eyes and my heart. Like a blind man with brand-new sight, I was seeing things for the very first time. I think the most interesting thing I realized was the fact that I was a complete and utter knucklehead. For those of you who may be unfamiliar with the species, Webster defines "knucklehead" as "a stupid person," Not too flattering for sure, but it's probably the nicest terminology I can think of when it comes to describing my overall attitude toward the women in my life. That is, before I met Hannah Jeanne.

I'm sure the women in my life up to that point would've used more descriptive language to describe my attitude than just "knucklehead." I had a mother, a sister, and an amazing wife who had just given birth to our beautiful daughter. But I was clueless when it came to understanding the relationship that God intended between men and women. I had no idea of the emotional, spiritual, or physical responsibilities that rested on my shoulders as a man, a son, a husband, and now the father of a daughter. I was utterly clueless.

Let me explain.

Even though my father had always taught me to respect women, there was something missing until I had a daughter of my own. Put another way, there was something that hadn't yet been birthed *in* me until a daughter had been birthed *to* me.

Don't get me wrong. I'm not trying to make excuses for my previous bad behavior toward women. Nor am I saying that in order for guys to learn to treat women right, they need to run out and have a daughter. I can only talk about my experience, my story. Hopefully, by reading this book, you will get a much-needed heads up so you can avoid following in my knuckleheaded footsteps.

Until the realization that came with Hannah's birth, I am embarrassed to say, women were mostly a means to an end. They were simply objects. I'm not saying I was a wild man, out every night purposely mistreating women, having random sexual hookups, hanging out in strip clubs, addicted to porn, involved in human trafficking, or habitually committing adultery. Don't get the wrong picture. But I have to confess that my attitude was one of a knucklehead, a stupid man, a dumbbell. And I can clearly see today that attitude was the seedbed where all other things start to grow. It was that knuckleheaded attitude that lies at the root of all evil things.

Here's what I mean. I had five basic foundational thoughts about women in general.

1. Women are prized, and they make you feel proud to be a man.

2. Women take care of the indoor housework, including the laundry and meal preparation.

3. Women are an integral part of the practice of sex.

4. Women are an integral part of the perpetuation of the species.

5. Lastly, if you want to take advantage of these principles regularly, you had better make sure you keep them happy at all costs. Always be prepared to give them gifts, and tell them what they want to hear. Don't tell them things that might upset them, even if it's the truth. Never forget, the phrase, "If Momma ain't happy, ain't nobody happy" didn't become part of our English lexicon and repeated millions of times every day for no reason. Everyone, or at least every man, knows this is true. Or at least they should.

There's my list. It's pretty hard for me to even put those words on the page, but there it is. Have you been able to figure out what's so knuckleheaded about my list? None of those things, taken on their own, is bad or wrong. Being proud of your wife, agreeing on who does what chores at home, having sex and making babies…none of those things are bad. They're great as a matter of fact. And so is the desire for the women in our lives to be happy.

So what makes my list so knuckleheaded? Do you see it? If you haven't picked up on it yet maybe you need help with your knuckleheadedness just as I did.

The answer of course is that the focus of my list—all five things, is me.

Look at the list again. There's nothing on that list that focuses on caring for a woman's heart. There's nothing about caring for her dreams, or her need for protection, or the fact that the women in our lives are wonderful gifts. There's no mention that all women are someone's daughter. Ultimately they are God's daughters. Think about it. Your mom, your sister, your daughter…every woman you can think of is someone's daughter. And they are all His daughters.

Let that sink in for a minute. Does that truth rattle your cage the way it rattled mine when I first realized it? Let me make it clearer and knucklehead-proof. It's not always about you! Stop being a knucklehead! You are not the center of the universe with everything and everyone revolving around you and whatever you want!

The women in your life are all daughters. They are precious and beautiful, and they all have the power to cause grown men—men just like you and me—to cry. More importantly, they are all God's daughters! They belong to Him. They cause His Father's heart to stir in a way no man's heart does. It's for this reason that they are to be treasured, admired, and cared for. They are not here for you to possess, to be used, or manipulated. There, did that clear things up for you? Is the knucklehead fog swirling around your head beginning to clear a little?

Now no matter what you may have heard, I'm not the father of all knuckleheads. I'm not the first man on this planet to have these thoughts. So if those thoughts didn't originate with me, where did they come from? Where did I get this immature, weak, and even primitive view of the male/female relationship?

Just like figuring out where I got my eye color, my personality, or facial characteristics, I got my views on women from my father. No…not my earthly father. His name was Kirk. My attitudes about women originated way before Kirk came along…before his father, or even before his father before him. I inherited those mistaken attitudes about women from the one who is ultimately father of us all: Adam.

Every single one of us are related to Adam, and we carry within us a slice of his DNA, which causes us to act or think as he did. Some of us have learned to hide that negative behavior better than others, but we all carry his genes. We can't escape or run away from the tendency to follow in his footsteps. In fact, unless we are able to renew our minds, we're destined to imitate Adam's destructive pattern. Our relationships with women will always be broken, never deep or fulfilling. We'll constantly be on a quest without ever finding the thing we're looking for, which is healthy relationships with the women in our lives. Without healing, we'll continue to treat women like possessions—as objects. And we'll ultimately crumple and fold like a cheap suit, just as Adam did.

Think of this book as a journey, and on this journey together we'll explore in depth the effects of Adam's sin and the way his sin continues to affect our lives even today, many generations later. Adam's great sin is called "The Fall," and it was The Fall that causes all of us to inherit Adam's fallen genetics.

The Fall is why I took women for granted, why I saw women only as objects orbiting around my world. Now before you get all smug about my fallen attitudes, admit it, you're the same way. You've taken women for granted too, and you've used them as objects. You want to know how I know? I know because you're a son of Adam, just as I am. Every man in this world at some point has followed in Adam's footsteps and objectified women. We've all failed to become the wall of protection and safety that God has called us to be in the lives of the women we hold dear.

But fortunately, there's help. God provided another Adam to correct what the first Adam messed up. Adam is referred to as "the First Adam" because there's another one, a second Adam. Yes, the First Adam was the father of all of us, the father of all knuckleheads. But thank God, there is another Adam who can help knuckleheads.

From Lori
Was Jeff really a knucklehead?

*W*hen Jeff and I got married, he was 22, and I was only 19. We were young, and we were in love. We loved Jesus with all our hearts, and we were ready to fulfill His calling in our lives and take on the world. The five statements that Jeff listed describing his attitude toward women were true. As we grow and mature, we have choices along the way to make changes in our attitudes and in our views toward one another. I've had a front row seat to witness firsthand the changes that Jeff has made in his attitude toward women. Jeff's love for me and his hunger to be the man God created him to be has literally changed the way he thinks and acts.

Jeff has always been a very passionate man—a man who goes after the things he wants in life. He's a visionary and a goal setter. He's able to fully put his mind to something and see it through all the way to the end. When Jeff and I were dating he had the most wonderful ways of making me feel like I was treasured. He made me feel like I was a gift from God. But all that shifted once we were married. Looking back now, it's easy to see his thought process. He'd pursued me in dating, and then he'd won me over in marriage. He had crossed the "marriage mission" off his list and was ready to put his sights on his next goal. I knew without a doubt that he was a good man, a godly man who loved Jesus with all his heart. But I was confused. His treatment of me, or more accurately, the way he thought about me had changed, and I wasn't sure what to do with that. To be honest I felt that my ranking in Jeff's world had fallen a notch or two. When we dated I felt confident that I was second, right behind Jesus. But after we were married things changed. While I was confident I was still in the top five, I knew I was no longer second. As you know, that's not God's model for a successful marriage!

Our first child, Jacob, was born in our fourth year of marriage. Jeff was so happy to have a son. He's already told you about signaling "touchdown" and dancing around the delivery room. It was a victory moment for both of us. I knew he felt a strong sense of fulfillment to have had a son.

Then, twenty months later another birth took place in our family. But this time it wasn't another son. I gave birth to our daughter, Hannah Jeanne. It was amazing to see the shift come over my husband. I knew in my heart that a father loves his sons differently than he loves his daughters. But to watch him in the moments after Hannah's birth was an incredible experience. There was no touchdown dance, no beating the chest, no rah-rahs. Just tears. Big, soft, gentle, tender tears rolling down Jeff's face, all the way down to his great big smile.

Hannah's birth marked a change in Jeff that would eventually cause his eyes to open. He began to see himself as more than just Hannah's father. He saw himself as a wall of protection, which was the very thing God had created him to be.

Today, over thirty-two years later, I look back over tough times and good times, and through it all, Jeff has taken his rightful place as a wall for our daughter and me. He has chosen to see us both the way our Heavenly Father sees and loves us, as His daughters, born with the desire for our voices to be heard, our hearts to be cared for, and our lives to be worth standing by and fighting for.

I'm so grateful to the Lord that our three sons have each learned from Jeff's example by watching him live a transparent life in front of us all. Our sons have watched Jeff's humility to make the necessary changes along the way. They've heard his words of repentance, forgiveness, and freedom, and seen his heart of humility. They've seen him live out his life as a wall through his intimate and deeply personal relationship with Christ. They've witnessed his practice of praying for us daily and speaking words of blessing over our lives.

They've also seen Jeff stand in the place God appointed for him, as a wall of strength and protection throughout some very crucial times in the life of our family. I have seen Jeff demonstrate the humility necessary to learn from our sons. Each of our boys is different. Each has his own personality and interacts differently to people and life's varied situations. I've watched Jeff learn incredible gentleness, forgiveness, and grace through the example set by our sons.

I'm grateful to the Lord that I've been able to witness firsthand the way the four brave Voth men of my household have learned to be a wall for His daughters.

A Masculine Wall #1
My Father: The First Wall I Ever Saw

The first wall I ever witnessed was my dad, Kirk Voth. But like most of us, he didn't start out being a wall. It was a skill he had to learn over time, a role he had to grow into. I'd have to say, when I was young, he probably tried to be an involved and caring father for my sister and me. I'm sure he thought he was doing his best to provide and protect my mom. But the fact is, by the time I was nine years old, my mom and dad were on the brink of a divorce.

Looking back, I was too young to understand the concept of divorce, but I was well aware of the tension in our home. My dad traveled for work a lot, leaving my mom to raise us on her own with very little help. She did her best, but my dad was simply never around during the week. He missed out on so much. And then when he was home, he wasn't present because he was so worn out from the work and the travel. Running after the American dream had him away from his family and his responsibilities at home.

I vividly remember when it all came crashing down. We were on a family vacation visiting some friends who owned a hotel in Gunnison, Colorado. I'll never know why he chose that time or that place to tell my mom, but it was on that trip, in our friends' hotel, that my dad informed my mom that he was leaving her…and us.

He tried to justify his decision by saying that they'd been growing apart for a while and it was time for him to start over someplace new. I'm not sure how he thought my mom would react, but I know he didn't expect the fury that followed. Not only did she not accept his decision, she got in his face and challenged him to step up, to show up, and to be a man for his family. She didn't use the word "wall," but she wanted him to be a wall for us. She made sure he knew that if he persisted in this foolishness that she was not going to take it quietly.

Faced with this amazing woman and her passion for family, my dad was immediately confronted with a choice. Would he crumple, tuck his tail, and run off, or would he stand fast, rise up, and start being a wall for his family? Ultimately he decided to be a wall, and fortunately he was smart enough to know that he was going to need some help. My dad understood that he had lost my mom's trust, and he was going to need God's help to rebuild it.

I thank God every day that my dad rose to the occasion and accepted my mom's challenge. I'm grateful that he reached out to that trustworthy Someone. Together in the car, with my sister and me in the backseat, my parents called out to Jesus. It was on the winding road passing over Monarch Pass in the Rocky Mountains of Colorado that my parents were saved. It was at that very moment that my dad began the process of becoming a wall for his family.

That process started with a prayer and a vow. The prayer was asking Jesus to save his marriage and family. His vow was to read through the Bible every year.

Both my earthly father and my Heavenly Father have made good on their promises for over forty years. My dad's love for and trust in the Word of God have changed his life, and that love and trust have both been passed on to his family. Our family was saved because my dad made a choice, the right choice. He chose to become a wall.

I witnessed my dad calling on God when his life had crumpled around his ankles. God built up my father through His Word, and my dad desired to follow Jesus with all his heart. His decision to become a wall for his family led to other positive decisions. He chose to stop traveling. He tended closely to the needs of my mom. He became an attentive father. He took us to church and taught us the ways of the Lord. My dad stepped up and showed up, and now, in his mid-seventies, he continues to faithfully care for my mom as she struggles with life-threatening health issues. My dad is the first wall I ever saw, and I'm grateful for him. It's because of my dad that I know what a wall looks like.

Question: *Who has been a wall for you? Write his or her name down, and say a prayer of thanks to God for that person. Send him or her a note, text, or email that you are thankful to God for his or her impact on your life.*

Chapter 2

Jesus Was Not a Knucklehead

But the gift is not like the trespass. For if the many died by the trespass of the one man [Adam], how much more did God's grace and the gift that came by the grace of the one man, Jesus Christ, overflow to the many!

—ROMANS 5:15

Jesus was not a knucklehead! How about that for a "no duh" statement? Jesus wasn't clueless like the first Adam, or like his many sons, grandsons, great grandsons, down through the ages. Jesus is our "second Adam." In the verse above, the Apostle Paul describes Jesus as a new, different kind of Adam, one who will bring hope for the fallen nature of men. I'm happy to inform you that in the person of Jesus Christ, there is hope for all us knuckleheads.

Needless to say, Jesus was perfect. He was spot on, focused, and clear when it came to the treatment of women. On the other hand, I was a knucklehead. I was only focused on me. I tended to take women for granted, to use them as objects in my life. But when Hannah Jeanne was born, she caused something to be born in me. I developed a whole new heart, a heart that finally began to understand that all women are daughters of God. He feels about His daughters the very same way I felt about Hannah. I understood that God sent His Son, Jesus, as a second Adam, to birth a whole new race of men, men who were willing to be a wall for His daughters—protective, strong, and faithful.

Let's take a closer look at the way Jesus treated women. We have a lot to learn from His example of "non-knuckleheaded" interactions with His daughters.

Jesus Didn't Troll

If you're a fisherman, you'll recognize the term quickly. Trolling is the technique of trailing fishing line with bait attached behind a slow-moving boat hoping to catch fish.

But of course there's another meaning. It's the slang term for moving slowly through a crowd hoping to pick up someone of the opposite sex. You get the analogy, right? Just like fishermen trolling in lakes and rivers, people have been trolling in bars and nightclubs, dance halls, and marketplaces for thousands of years.

In fact, as I read through the interaction in John 4 of Jesus and the woman at the well, I'm convinced that she was trolling…and I think He was too. But Jesus was trolling for a completely different reason.

> *Now he [Jesus] had to go through Samaria. So he came to a town in Samaria called Sychar, near the plot of ground Jacob had given to his son Joseph. Jacob's well was there, and Jesus, tired as he was from the journey, sat down by the well. It was about noon.*
>
> *When a Samaritan woman came to draw water, Jesus said to her, "Will you give me a drink?" (His disciples had gone into the town to buy food.)*
>
> *The Samaritan woman said to him, "You are a Jew and I am a Samaritan woman. How can you ask me for a drink?" (For Jews do not associate with Samaritans.)*
>
> *Jesus answered her, "If you knew the gift of God and who it is that asks you for a drink, you would have asked him and he would have given you living water."*

"Sir," the woman said, "you have nothing to draw with and the well is deep. Where can you get this living water? Are you greater than our father Jacob, who gave us the well and drank from it himself, as did also his sons and his livestock?"

Jesus answered, "Everyone who drinks this water will be thirsty again, but whoever drinks the water I give them will never thirst. Indeed, the water I give them will become in them a spring of water welling up to eternal life."

The woman said to him, "Sir, give me this water so that I won't get thirsty and have to keep coming here to draw water."

He told her, "Go, call your husband and come back."

"I have no husband," she replied.

Jesus said to her, "You are right when you say you have no husband. The fact is, you have had five husbands, and the man you now have is not your husband. What you have just said is quite true."

—JOHN 4:4–18

Wow. When you consider the trolling angle, you can see that she was really putting it out there. She had done this before and had perfected the art of trolling. Now before you freak out about this way to view the passage, think about it for just a minute. Don't be closed-minded. Think outside the box. Jesus had stopped at a place predominantly frequented by women, right? They were the primary gatherers of water. I can't help but think that there were not many places better to pick up a woman. And it's not like a bar; you could have a perfectly logical reason to be there if your friends or family happened to see you at the well. Obviously, Jesus was not there trolling for a date. But the woman had no way of knowing that.

If you've gone to church as long as I have, you get used to reading these passages front-loaded with so many assumptions. But read through it again with fresh eyes. Maybe even pretend you're reading this story not knowing it's in the Bible. It's easy to see, especially through fallen eyes and attitudes that this chance meeting could've been a prelude to a whole different kind of encounter.

As you read through those verses, it's obvious that she was pretty well traveled when it came to men. Certainly she had been objectified throughout her life. Jesus reads her mail, confronting her with the fact that she had been with at least five men and was currently shacking up with a sixth. With all that in mind, it's not a stretch to think that she assumed that Jesus was just like any other man trolling for women that afternoon at the well. Sadly, that's what her life experience had trained her to think.

But what she didn't realize at the time was that Jesus wasn't desiring a hookup. He was trolling in a different way, desiring a different result. He was trolling for her soul, not her body. He was patiently fishing for her soul, because He knew how valuable she was in God's eyes. She was His daughter. Take a closer look at His strategy:

- First, He lured her in with a baited question, one that she probably assumed was a pick-up line, "Will you give Me a drink?" But, as we know, He wasn't talking about physical water; He wasn't trolling for physical things. He was patiently trolling for her soul. He wasn't asking for anything from her, He wanted to satisfy her soul, not her body. She bit. "How can You ask me for a drink?"

- Second, He piques her interest by engaging her in a conversation about a different kind of water. He told her about eternal, spiritual water that causes you to never thirst again. Finally, she takes the bait. "Sir, give me this water."

Boom! The hook is set, and she's on the line. He begins to reel her in, proving to her that He is a man who doesn't troll like other men. He asks her about her husband, and she starts trolling in a way that she has spent a lifetime perfecting. She lies. She tells Him what she thinks He wants to hear. She tells Him she has no husband. It's at this point I'm convinced that she thought she had set a hook of her own. I mean, read it. She was putting it out there.

But look closely. Jesus doesn't bite, as so many other men had before. With her past success rate, she had to be surprised when she didn't hook Him with that bait. And not only did He not take the bait, He was able to see into her dark places and combat her lie with the truth of her past.

She is shocked and claims that He must be a prophet. In her confusion, she shrugs her shoulders and tells Jesus that when the Messiah comes, everything will be explained.

I imagine in that moment Jesus looked into her eyes and smiled. He told her that He *is* the Messiah, the One she's been waiting for. Immediately she understands. She thought He was trolling for her in one way but now she realizes He was after something completely different. He was after her soul.

She gets so flustered that she leaves her water pots, runs home, gets saved on the way, evangelizes her town, and then brings them back to meet Jesus. All of this happened because Jesus chose not to troll like other men. He wasn't after her because of what she could give to Him. He only wanted to give her the Living Water, eternal life.

This interaction with the woman at the well is one of my favorites in the entire Bible. I want to be able to troll like this. I pray that God would help all of us men to troll like Jesus, not after bodies but souls. May the Lord help us seek after the hearts and souls of women, without becoming fixated on their bodies or pursuing them only because of what they can do for us.

Stop right now, and ask Jesus to teach you to troll like He does.

He Didn't Peep Like That

There's another situation I want to show you where Jesus's non-knuckleheaded nature runs contrary to other men. This one has to do with His response to a bunch of religious, self-righteous, peeping toms who had caught a woman in the act of committing adultery.

> *But Jesus went to the Mount of Olives.*
>
> *At dawn he appeared again in the temple courts, where all the people gathered around him, and he sat down to teach them. The teachers of the law and the Pharisees brought in a woman caught in adultery. They made her stand before the group and said to Jesus, "Teacher, this woman was caught in the act of adultery. In the Law Moses commanded us to stone such women. Now what do you say?" They were using this question as a trap, in order to have a basis for accusing him.*

> *But Jesus bent down and started to write on the ground with his finger. When they kept on questioning him, he straightened up and said to them, "Let any one of you who is without sin be the first to throw a stone at her." Again he stooped down and wrote on the ground.*
>
> *At this, those who heard began to go away one at a time, the older ones first, until only Jesus was left, with the woman still standing there. Jesus straightened up and asked her, "Woman, where are they? Has no one condemned you?"*
>
> *"No one, sir," she said.*
>
> *"Then neither do I condemn you," Jesus declared. "Go now and leave your life of sin."*
>
> —JOHN 8:1–11

Okay, I'll be the first to admit, this is weird on several different levels. Remember, if you've grown up in the church as I have, we've read this story many times before. We are able to jump ahead to see what a holy moment this turned out to be. But when you read through it again, with fresh eyes, forgetting that it's Scripture, it's easier to put a whole new spin on this passage, to see these verses in a new light, a new understanding.

First of all, the text says that she was caught in adultery, caught "in the act." Okay, now let's think about this for a minute. How did those guys know where and when she was going to be having sex with a man who was not her husband? You know they weren't having sex right out in plain sight! The couple was probably sneaking around, thinking they had found some privacy. But someone had been spying. A deal must've been made. A secret time and place must've been shared with others. Being forewarned, the religious were ready with front row seats.

Since the couple needed to be caught in the act, someone must've been peeking in the window. Obviously, this was before the day of hidden cameras. They had to resort to the old school way of peeking in the window. Maybe there was a crowd of them huddled outside the door listening. Yeah, I know. Weird, and perverted. These religious voyeurs were straight up sick and wrong. They were using this couple (or at least the woman; more on the man in a minute) caught in sexual sin to entrap Jesus.

Secondly, why do you suppose these guys insisted on embarrassing the girl in front of a crowd? Look again at the story. This woman was caught in the act, then dragged through the street to where Jesus was teaching a crowd of people. These sick perverts insisted on throwing her, half clothed, maybe wrapped in a blanket, down in front of the Rabbi. How embarrassing would that be? How hurtful and shameful would it be? These were nothing but peeping, religious knuckleheads, bent on intimidation.

They thought they were going to be able to back Jesus into a corner, to catch Him off guard. Those knuckleheads didn't give a rip about the girl. She was a piece of trash to them. Like other knuckleheads before them, they were just using this woman as a means to an end. They had set her up and then kidnapped her for their own purposes. The statement, "They *made* her stand before the group…" only proves that she was being taken there against her will. These men were no more than religious pimps, human traffickers.

Finally, where was the guy in all this? I mean it takes two to tango, right? So where was the other tango-er? How hypocritical can you get? When I read this passage, it looks like it was a total setup from the start. These knuckleheads had the dirt on both the girl and the guy, but did nothing about the guy's involvement. Dirty. Sexist. Religious.

I'm convinced because of those reasons Jesus did what He did next.

First, He crouched down and began to write something in the dirt with His finger. This act alone took the attention away from the woman. In that instant, all eyes were on Jesus. Symbolically, He was acting as a wall, shielding her from their prying eyes and accusations. By drawing their attention away from her He was covering her shame.

The verse says that He wrote on the ground with His finger. Down through time there's been a lot of speculation about what He wrote. The fact is, no one knows for sure. I'd like to think He was spelling out the sins of the knuckleheads who had dragged this poor woman through town. While He was effectively covering her sin, He was revealing theirs by writing their dirt in the dirt. Chances are, there were others who had been victimized by this religious mob before. They knew Jesus was right. They all knew these guys were dirty.

Next, Jesus rose to His full height and stared at them in their guilty faces. I imagine Him looking down at what He'd written in the dirt and looking back at them and saying, "If any of you is without sin, let him be the first to throw a stone at her." *Boom!* They thought they were making this all about the woman and her sin, but Jesus completely turned the tables and made it all about them and their sins!

Like a wall, Jesus deflected the guilt and shame they meant to use as a weapon against the woman. The guilt and shame now rained down on them through the truth of Jesus's pointed statement. In that moment, Jesus had become a wall for His daughter.

Not one of them could so much as pick up a pebble. They were frozen. While they were trying to figure a way out of that awkward moment, Jesus bent back down and continued to write in the dirt. Eventually, the self-righteous mob of knuckleheads dispersed. Ironically, they were chased away by the only One present worthy of actually picking up a stone and hurling it at the woman, the only One present without sin. But instead of picking up a stone, He became a stone, a whole manly wall of stones.

Jesus wasn't about peeping and sneaking around trying to catch people in dirty traps. He preferred to look them straight in the eye with a look that at the same time chased away religious traffickers while comforting a hurting woman. Comforted, covered, protected, loved, and sent off to live a better life. This woman, and millions like her down through time, was someone's daughter. She was His daughter.

I pray that God would help us all get rid of those ugly ways we relate to women. No more peeping, hoping for a perverted momentary thrill. No more objectifying, manipulating, or using. I pray that we would be moved by the Holy Spirit to step in front of women, to be a wall of covering and protection, creating a safe place where they can live, grow, love, and hope.

He Didn't Touch Like That

Although there are many more examples I could cite from Scripture, there is one more I want to tell you about. Like the others, it describes an encounter that Jesus had with a troubled woman, struggling under the weight of many years of oppression by men.

When one of the Pharisees invited Jesus to have dinner with him, he went to the Pharisee's house and reclined at the table. A woman in that town who lived a sinful life learned that Jesus was eating at the Pharisee's house, so she came there with an alabaster jar of perfume. As she stood behind him at his feet weeping, she began to wet his feet with her tears. Then she wiped them with her hair, kissed them and poured perfume on them.

When the Pharisee who had invited him saw this, he said to himself, "If this man were a prophet, he would know who is touching him and what kind of woman she is—that she is a sinner."

Jesus answered him, "Simon, I have something to tell you."

"Tell me, teacher," he said.

"Two people owed money to a certain moneylender. One owed him five hundred denarii, and the other fifty. Neither of them had the money to pay him back, so he forgave the debts of both. Now which of them will love him more?"

Simon replied, "I suppose the one who had the bigger debt forgiven."

"You have judged correctly," Jesus said.

Then he turned toward the woman and said to Simon, "Do you see this woman? I came into your house. You did not give me any water for my feet, but she wet my feet with her tears and wiped them with her hair. You did not give me a kiss, but this woman, from the time I entered, has not stopped kissing my feet. You did not put oil on my head, but she has poured perfume on my feet. Therefore, I tell you, her many sins have been forgiven—as her great love has shown. But whoever has been forgiven little loves little."

Then Jesus said to her, "Your sins are forgiven."

The other guests began to say among themselves, "Who is this who even forgives sins?"

Jesus said to the woman, "Your faith has saved you; go in peace."

—LUKE 7:36–50

I am going to be straight up honest with you; this seems a little bit weird, maybe even somewhat erotic. Remember, don't react right away. Take your time and read through the passage again without your preconceived notions of what you've learned that the story is about. If you read about the behavior of this woman, it's pretty brash. She comes right in the house and elbows her way past the religious and community leaders of the day. She's immediately recognized as a prostitute. She wears her hair down, and her head is uncovered, both a dead giveaway. Proper women of the day would never consider appearing in public without a veil. They would always keep their heads covered when they were out and around town.

This woman, full of passion and emotion, threw herself at the feet of Jesus. She was intentional and full of purpose. She was on a mission to get to Jesus. She was focused. She didn't consider her surroundings at all. She was oblivious to the looks of judgment that were coming her way from all quarters of the room.

There's nothing more attractive to a man than a woman who is focused on him, right? It'd be hard to resist a woman who is so completely consumed with you. I mean, admit it, what red-blooded American man wouldn't get at least a little bit excited by a woman kissing, rubbing, and crying all over his feet, then drying them with her hair? I know, it's tough to imagine. But calm down and stay with me. Maybe it's just me, but I think this is pretty erotic, and I can see where it could fire up almost any guy. Remember, this girl had a reputation. I'm sure it was easy for the men present to toy with the idea of the things that could happen if they could only spend some private time with her later.

Okay. I know. This is pretty "out there" to think about. I know I might be skating on thin ice, turning a beautiful salvation encounter into something sexually sinful. I'm embarrassed to admit that my mind even went there, but I'm trying to be honest with you and look at this story from the perspective of a knucklehead. And believe me, I have plenty of experience thinking like a knucklehead!

This is how so many of us guys have the potential to think. Many times that's where our mind immediately goes, objectification, power, sex, and selfish oppression. You're a guy. Admit it. How often have you thought about something dirty even in the most innocent of situations? We're knuckleheads! We can turn anything into something about sex. This is where we live. This is the bold-faced, unredeemed nature of the alpha male. That's why we all need Jesus so desperately, to save us from ourselves and our knuckleheaded nature.

The truth is, we'll never be free unless we're delivered from that nature. Remember where we got it? Our earthly father and his genetic makeup, passed down the line from the first Adam. We need Jesus to break the chain. We need Him to save us from that old nature and those old thought patterns. We need Him to replace those with a whole new nature, one that doesn't view women as objects for us to use however we see fit.

But you know Jesus. He is no knucklehead, not then and not now. Sure, He was as focused on the woman as she was on Him, but He wasn't thinking about sex. Far from it. He was all about saving souls and healing hearts. Like the other women we've talked about, Jesus knew with one look—the hurt, the pain, the anguish that she lived with every single day. Her need touched Him deeply, and He longed to ease her pain. But to do that, He was going to have to reach out and touch her, which was unthinkable to the other men in the room.

Touch assumes closeness. Touch means proximity. And things happen when men and women get close and touch. Heck, who am I kidding. Men often don't even need to touch something. Usually all it takes is just an image in their mind. It's part of the knuckleheaded nature we inherited from Adam.

But remember, Jesus is the second Adam. He came to redeem the things that Adam got wrong, including the way he viewed women. Jesus can help us renew our minds. How? Jesus was a man. He had the same genetic makeup as we do. He had the capability to think sexual, sensual thoughts. But unlike us, He never ever sinned. The writer of the Book of Hebrews reminds us,

> For we do not have a high priest who is unable to empathize with our weaknesses, but we have one who has been tempted in every way, just as we are—yet he did not sin.
>
> —HEBREWS 4:15

Thank you, Jesus! He was tempted to sin but never did. Let me say it again. Jesus was tempted, just as we are. But He never sinned! He did not objectify women. He did not touch them sinfully. He did not fantasize about them. He lived a perfect, healthy, balanced, manly, and sinless life. He is the perfect One to give us the capacity to live in that victory just as He did.

With His resurrection, He sealed the ultimate victory over everything that would ever plague the masculine body, soul, and spirit. Jesus saves our entire nature, including the way we think and interact with women. That includes our mothers, our wives, our female coworkers, women on computer screens, women in church services, and women walking down the street.

If you've struggled in this area as I have, you should fall on your knees right this minute and ask Jesus to save you and ask Him to give you His heart for all women. When this happens, and it will happen if you ask for it, you will receive a whole new nature. You'll gain not just a new way of thinking; you'll gain a new way of being. Remember what the Apostle Paul said:

> *Therefore, if anyone is in Christ, the new creation has come: The old has gone, the new is here!*
>
> —2 CORINTHIANS 5:17

Let's look again at exactly how Jesus treats the woman in Luke 7. He treats her with dignity and respect. He allows her to come close and even touch Him, despite her reputation. Most importantly, He becomes a wall for her, defending her actions to the religious knuckleheads in the room. He saves her. He takes her face in His healing hands and says, "Your sins are forgiven. Your faith has saved you; go in peace." With that touch, He made her into a new creation, all new, with none of the old nature.

In a knuckleheaded approach, a touch is more like a grab, taking what it wants and using it for sinful, selfish pleasure. But when your mind is renewed and your nature has been changed, touch is a healthy and healing thing, something that brings life and not death. Learning when and how to touch and learning when and how not to touch women is something Jesus can teach all of us men. The story in Luke 7 is a great example.

Take it from a guy who's been there. You can be delivered from your knuckleheaded nature. Your mind can be renewed in this area. And as you know, if you get your mind right, the right actions will follow. And when your actions are right, your life can change. This kind of change is especially important in the midst of a hyper-sexualized, voyeuristic culture.

If we ever hope to be the wall of non-knuckleheaded manhood that God created us to be, we're going to have to pattern our lives and our nature after His. We must learn to touch others the way He touched them, with humility and healing, not with selfish intent.

> Lord Jesus, I ask You to teach us to reach out and touch the women in our lives the way that You would have us touch them. I pray that we would learn to love, honor, and respect them the way You do, because they are Your daughters, they are Your Daddy's girls.

From Lori

How did Jesus "touch" you through the men in your life?

On our wedding day, Jeff committed his life to me with vows that he has lived out faithfully. Throughout our marriage, he has continued to make the necessary changes in his thinking for me, our marriage, and our family. He is careful to serve me with pure intentions, hearing from God on our behalf about our present situations as well as our future together. He embraces all of life while remaining diligent to speak life to me daily. He leads our home. He believes in me and encourages me. He loves me so well.

Growing up, my dad was so good to provide me with many opportunities for growth and learning. These opportunities have proven time and time again to be of great value. He taught me to love people—all people—regardless of their background. He taught me to value them and treat them with dignity. He gave me responsibilities that allowed me to use my gifts at an early age. This gave me the chance to hone my natural gifts into skills I would need later in life. Above all, I know my dad trusted me. This made me feel valued and treasured.

I was one of four sisters to my older (and only) brother. When I was a teenager, I remember him telling me to be careful when choosing who to date. He told me that God had someone special, a godly man, to be my husband someday. I always knew my brother cared for me. His attention, his words, and his time not only meant a lot to me, they made me feel safe.

Through the years I had the blessing of having a few male teachers and administrators who, now looking back, I see acted as a wall in my life. Their presence in my life made me feel protected and safe anytime I was around them. They cared about who I dated, where I would go to college, and who I would marry. They even told me about the guys I should stay away from! Their attitudes toward me covered me and protected me, making me feel safe.

My Pappo was an exemplary man who loved people with great excellence. From as early as I can remember, when he talked to me, it was as if I were the only person in the room. His focus gave me the wonderful feeling that he delighted in my presence.

My father-in-law was intentional about welcoming me into the family, always telling me how proud he was to have me as his daughter-in-law. He has consistently spoken blessings over me for more than 32 years.

My oldest son expresses the love of Jesus by loving his wife well. How does that affect me? It blesses me to see him be a blessing to his wife. Watching Jacob get married was more than just a ceremony. It was a transition, in his life and in mine. I stepped down so that his wife could step in and take over the first place in his life. To me, it seemed a natural part of God's design and order. To this day, Jacob tells me how much that meant to him that I was willing to step aside for his wife. That blesses me.

My middle and youngest sons, Caleb and Cody, demonstrate Jesus's love for me by honoring me, respecting me, and loving me. They do these things, not just when people are watching, but also when no one is around. They go out of their way often to express their care for me, being very intentional with sustaining the special relationship we have.

My son-in-law, Mark, blesses me by opening his home and his family (including our grandchildren) to me. I'm blessed that my daughter doesn't have to choose between her new family and the family she grew up in. My son-in-law is quick to welcome me when I am around him, and when he speaks to me it's with such love and respect. This blesses me. He loves our daughter and has made the decision to be a wall for her, which is the greatest blessing a parent could ever ask for.

Finally, I'm grateful to Jesus. He has touched me in a deep and profound way through the men He has placed in my life. Through their actions on my behalf, Jesus has shown that He is a wall for me.

A Masculine Wall #2
A Homeless Wall

Francisco Erasmo Rodrigues de Lima is a name I'm sure you've never heard before. You've never heard of him because he was one of Brazil's anonymous homeless men, living out his life on the streets of Sao Paulo. But on a day in September of 2015, Francisco became much more than just a homeless man. He became a wall of strength and protection for a helpless woman.

Francisco was seeking relief from the oppressive midday heat by waiting for a free meal in the cool shadows outside the world famous Sao Paulo Cathedral. While in the shadows minding his own business, he heard a woman scream. He turned to see a woman being accosted and robbed while she prayed in the churchyard.

The attacker was a career criminal who had served much of his life in jail for various crimes. He saw the innocent woman focused in prayer and made her his target. He almost got away with it. That is until an anonymous homeless man decided to become a wall of protection. Francisco rushed to her defense. He was able to keep the attacker busy until authorities arrived, saving the woman but paying a steep price.

It'd be great to hear Francisco's side of the story. What was he thinking? What motivated him to rush to the woman's aid? We'll never know the answers to those questions. Francisco was shot and killed while scuffling with the attacker. He gave up his life doing what walls do. He stood. He stepped out of the shade and into the light and was transformed from an anonymous homeless man to a giant, a hero, a wall of protection for a nameless woman. He took the shots and died so that she could go free. What an example for all of us.[1]

Why is it that stories like this move us so much? I believe it is because stories like this express the heart of the Father toward His daughters. Francisco was working on behalf of God, protecting one of His daughters even at the cost of his own life. This is the true heart of Jesus. This is how we should act and think. Jesus, please help us be like Francisco who was willing to be like You.

> **Question:** *While you probably will never have to do what Francisco did in order to be a wall for the women in your world, take some time right now to think about a couple of practical ways in which you might come to their rescue. How would you respond?*

∞ Section 2 ∞
The Masculine Wall

"A wall of men, instead of bricks, is best."[1]

—LYCURGUS

This section is an indictment as to just how low and degraded the wall of men and masculinity in our culture has become. We'll explore a foundational new strategy of how we can change our crippled status. God's original design was for the men of every family and of every culture to rise up and stand as a wall of protection against the attacks of the enemy. In God's design, it's the men who are to be the wall that makes people safe. Needless to say, things have gone downhill since Creation, and today's reality bears little resemblance to God's original design. The masculine wall that once existed is no longer present in our culture like it used to be. This wall has been assaulted, beaten upon, and broken down. In this section of the book, I will explore how and why this is so, and then I will provide some strategies of how we might not just rebuild the wall, but build a brand-new one.

Chapter 3

The Ancient Wall

Holy walls of manly protection and defense don't seem to exist much anymore. At least not like they did in the ancient world. Our current culture is too civilized, too "politically correct." Maybe we think we don't need walls of protection. Maybe the walls of protection and security have become virtual. Instead of relying on actual walls of stone our culture has become reliant on electronics. Cities have gotten too big to be protected by walls.

Who will ever forget 9/11? If anything, that day proved that we are vulnerable to attack. Since that day, we've become complacent. In many ways, we've become so sophisticated in our own minds we think we can protect ourselves and we don't need any help from anyone or anything. I think it's more likely that we've resigned ourselves to living in fear. We've given up on the whole idea that we can even be protected. There is no such thing as 100 percent security. Just take a look around. Millions of people are living in fear, afraid that at any given moment something bad is going to happen.

I personally think it's all crap. Yeah, you heard me. I said crap. I used that word on purpose because that's what it is. And it's really a nicer word than the one I wanted to use, a whole big pile of it too.

Bottom line? Don't be misled by the political correctness of our current culture. We all need walls, every last one of us. In this day and age, we probably don't need walls made of brick and stone. But our culture is desperate for living, breathing, masculine walls like the one God put in the Garden to begin with. God designed Adam to be a wall to stand for and protect His daughter. But, as we saw in the first chapter, Adam blew it. He blew it astronomically.

Are there walls anymore? As you look around today do you see a protective shield anywhere? Maybe…if you look really close. But it wasn't always that way.

In the Bible, especially in the Old Testament, we read a lot about walls. Much of the time the walls are descriptive of God's protective heart toward His people. Take the word *bulwark* for instance. Don't you love that word? I love words that sound like what they actually mean.

A bulwark is a solid wall-like structure raised for defense. It's often a system of two walls with space between. God's salvation was known as a bulwark for His people.[1]

In the Psalms, David declares,

> *Through the praise of children and infants you have established a* strong-hold [bulwark] *against your enemies, to silence the foe and the avenger.*
> —PSALM 8:2, COMMENTARY AND EMPHASIS ADDED

The prophet Isaiah affirms…

> *We have a* strong city [bulwark]*; God makes salvation its walls and ramparts.*
> —ISAIAH 26:1, COMMENTARY AND EMPHASIS ADDED

Another great word is *rampart*. A rampart is an outer ring of fortifications, usually mounds of dirt and rocks. The Hebrew term literally means "encirclement" and can consist of moats, walls, and mounds. Jerusalem, God's holy city, was ringed by steep valleys on one side and ramparts on the other.

> *Peace be within your walls, and security within your* towers [ramparts]!
> —PSALM 122:7, NRSV, COMMENTARY AND EMPHASIS ADDED

The "towers" were a set of walls that could be inhabited and were built for added strength and protection at potentially weak spots in the main wall, such as corners, gateways, or openings for water supplies. The towers had inner access stairways and chambers for use by soldiers who manned the structures and for watchmen who announced the approach of danger. On the outside there were gates with massive piers and bronze or iron bars and bolts. These gates were hung on pivots driven into the pavement below and into the lintel above, strongly fortified and carefully protected.

The "fortified" or "fenced city" referred to a town with strong defenses, usually a massive walled structure with inner citadels or strongholds.[2]

> Today I have made you a fortified city, *an iron pillar and a bronze wall to stand against the whole land—against the kings of Judah, its officials, its priests and the people of the land.*
> —JEREMIAH 1:18, EMPHASIS ADDED

All of these images from Scripture and many, many more create powerful pictures in our mind. These are metaphors that convey what God wants to be for His people and, if the truth were told, for all the people of the world. You think He's trying to make a point here? Do you see a common thread that runs throughout all the verses above? I sure do. These verses, and there are many others too, show that God is crying out to us that He is our *bulwark, fortress, rampart, walled city,* and *high tower.*

He is a sure strength and protection for those who love Him. It makes me feel safe just saying these things. At the same time I'm dreadfully concerned that people don't really seem to care much anymore. As I look around today, I don't see much concern at the lack of protective walls available to us. There seems to be no concern at all that critical walls are missing from our government, our churches, our cities, our homes, and in our relationships with each other.

In Scripture, the prophets realized that the strength and defense of a nation was not in fortifications of brick and stone, but in God Himself. In their writings they urged the people for thousands of years to put their trust in the Lord as a secure refuge and wall of protection.

The LORD is my rock, my fortress and my deliverer;...He is my stronghold, my refuge and my savior—from violent people you save me.
—2 SAMUEL 22:2–3, EMPHASIS ADDED

The way of the LORD is a refuge for the blameless, but it is the ruin of those who do evil.
—PROVERBS 10:29, EMPHASIS ADDED

You have been a refuge for the poor, a refuge for the needy in their distress, a shelter from the storm and a shade from the heat. For the breath of the ruthless is like a storm driving against a wall.
—ISAIAH 25:4, EMPHASIS ADDED

LORD, my strength and my fortress, my refuge in time of distress, to you the nations will come from the ends of the earth and say, "Our ancestors possessed nothing but false gods, worthless idols that did them no good."
—JEREMIAH 16:19, EMPHASIS ADDED

The LORD is good, a refuge in times of trouble. He cares for those who trust in him.
—NAHUM 1:7, EMPHASIS ADDED

The LORD will roar from Zion and thunder from Jerusalem; the earth and the heavens will tremble. But the LORD will be a refuge for his people, a stronghold for the people of Israel.
—JOEL 3:16, EMPHASIS ADDED

So, as you can see, in the ancient world of Scripture a wall was more than just a wall; it was a sacred and holy thing. A wall was the thing that brought definition to a city. It was the wall that defined its borders and made the city safe from outside forces bent on destruction.

The famous French historian Numa Denis Fustel de Coulanges points out that in many cultures it was an offense to even touch the sacred wall surrounding a city without the permission of the presiding religious authorities. A holy wall of protection is under the jurisdiction of God. He maintained that the wall is an image of God, put there by Him, a holy Wall, put there by the Wall Himself.[3] Wow. That's quite a powerful picture.

In city after city across our great nation, buildings that once stood tall and proud are sagging or falling down. Their windows are shattered, their walls are crumbling, and whatever is left standing is tagged by graffiti. Whole neighborhoods, once thriving and vibrant, are now abandoned and forgotten. Detroit is no longer the industrial giant it once was with bustling city streets and vibrant neighborhoods full of hard working families. Today, Detroit struggles to figure out what to do with thousands and thousands of vacant structures.[4] Those vibrant neighborhoods are just a distant memory.

The same thing is happening in Chicago, Philadelphia, and Baltimore. I was in one major city and saw with my own eyes the walls of abandoned buildings and houses, riddled with gang tags, forgotten by everyone but the gang members who were squatting there. As I processed the desolation, a thought hit me like a ton of bricks from the war room of Heaven:

> Those trashed walls and broken down buildings are like the lives of so many men I know. In fact, they are like the state of masculinity throughout our whole culture. Forgotten. Riddled with weird, sometimes vile and profane pictures. Words that only a few people can understand. Unattended. Unwanted by some, home turf to others, but desperately needed by everyone. A once proud wall of masculinity is now abandoned, defaced, scarred, and left to rot and deteriorate.

The current state of manhood in our culture is like the crumbling walls of inner city neighborhoods.

Cultural commentator Luke Manley (yes, that's his real name) says it this way,

> When you reflect on what it means to be a Man, you probably think in much the same way as generations of men have before you. The tough Western cowboy, the dutiful soldier, or the heroic fireman. Chances are you don't consider Adam Sandler's Billy Madison, Seth McFarlane's Peter Griffin, or any of the current crop of male TV sitcom characters to be pillars of Masculinity. Yet while the stoic, focused, and responsible male archetype has persisted for generations,

it seems that at no other point in our history has the reality deviated so sharply from the ideal.

…Most frightening of all is that the statistics bear out this shift. Surely exacerbated by the current financial crisis, which has hit men especially hard, a staggering 55% of American men between 18 and 24 years old and 13% between 25 and 34 are currently living with their parents. This is compared to only 8% of women in the same situation. The average age for marriage has been climbing steadily over the years and now over 16 percent of men reach their early 40s without marrying, up from only 6% in 1980. What do the statistics say men are doing with all this extra time? Sadly, not working on their careers, but rather indulging in the same activities that they were unable to leave behind in college. For example, the average video game player was 18 years old a decade ago. Want to take a guess at the mean age now? If you guessed 33 you would be sadly correct.[5]

Are you kidding me? Partying like the guys in *Animal House* and playing video games is not the way grown men act, especially men who are supposed to be walls, standing fast and protective. But the indictment against the status of masculinity in our culture only gets worse.

According to David Blakenhorn, author of *Fatherless America*[6] along with research conducted by Paul Popenoe as well as scores of others cite some staggering statistics:

- Fatherless children are at a dramatically greater risk of drug and alcohol abuse, mental illness, suicide, poor educational performance, teen pregnancy, and criminality, according to the U.S. Department of Health and Human Services, National Center for Health Statistics.

- Over half of all children living with a single mother are living in poverty, a rate 5 to 6 times that of kids living with both parents.

- Child abuse is significantly more likely to occur in single parent homes than in intact families.

- Sixty-three percent of youth suicides are from fatherless homes according to the U.S. Bureau of the Census.

- Seventy-two percent of adolescent murderers grew up without fathers. Sixty percent of America's rapists grew up the same way according to a study by D. Cornell (et. al.), in *Behavioral Sciences and the Law.*

- Seventy-one percent of all high school dropouts come from father-less homes according to the National Principals Association Report on the State of High Schools.

- Eighty percent of rapists motivated with displaced anger come from fatherless homes according to a report in Criminal Justice & Behavior.

- In single-mother families in the U.S. about 66% of young children live in poverty.

- Ninety percent of all homeless and runaway children are from fatherless homes.

- Children from low-income, two-parent families outperform students from high-income, single-parent homes. Almost twice as many high achievers come from two-parent homes as from one-parent homes according to a study by the Charles F. Kettering Foundation.

- Eighty-five percent of all children that exhibit behavioral disorders come from fatherless homes according to a study by the Center for Disease Control.

- Girls living with non-natal fathers (boyfriends and stepfathers) are at higher risk for sexual abuse than girls living with natal fathers.

- The Scholastic Aptitude Test scores have declined more than 70 points in the past two decades; children in single-parent families tend to score lower on standardized tests and to receive lower grades in school according to a Congressional Research Service Report.

America is facing not just the loss of fathers, but also the erosion of the ideal of fatherhood. Few people doubt the fundamental importance of mothers…but increasingly the question of whether fathers are really necessary is being raised and said by many to be merely a social role that others—mothers, partners, stepfathers, uncles and aunts, and grandparents—can play.[7]

The social scientists quoted above are only two voices in a long line of observers who know that something is wrong, drastically wrong. As we sit by and watch, our culture is imploding, and it's clear that the enemy is at the gates. In fact, the enemy doesn't even need to try and storm the gates; he can simply waltz through the massive, gaping holes in the walls. The wall of manhood has been desecrated, vandalized, and, in many places, lies in heaps of rubble. Yet I can't think of another time in history when the wall of manhood has been more desperately needed.

From Lori

How have you seen your sons assaulted by cultural definitions of what manhood should be?

*H*aving three sons has been a blessing. I sure love my "boys." I have always loved and been intrigued by their unique personalities. It's weird, they have the same mother and father yet they are different in so many ways. I love it. It's these differences that make us better as a family. Embracing their unique qualities and personalities has not always been easy. Our culture and society influence all of us at every turn. With no walls to protect us, the enemy has been allowed not only to gain an entrance but also to run roughshod over our families, and more specifically our men.

Men today are bombarded with messages designed to skew and distort a man's true purpose. I'm sure you've been aware of these destructive messages:

- A man is just an animal. He can't help the way he acts.
- Real men don't cry.

- A man must be an athlete.
- A man can't be interested in music or the arts.
- A man should never admit his weaknesses.
- A man should always have the right answer.
- A man has to be a certain height and weight.

Imagine all these messages, and many more, walking through the door of your home every day. I have a husband and three sons. Believe me, I'm well aware of the affect these cultural lies have on our men.

As with all parents, there are a few things I probably would have changed in raising my sons. All of us struggle with those kinds of regrets from time to time. But to this day, I'm careful to tell them that I did the very best I knew how with the knowledge I had at the time. What I can see clearly now that I wasn't sure of then is the importance of taking a stand against the assault coming at my men every single day. I am offended that the enemy would ever try to take one of my men out through his lies and deceptions about their masculinity.

Ladies, it's our responsibility to build up our men with words and actions. We need to remember to speak to and encourage them in their masculinity, not to build an arrogant and domineering giant like Goliath, but to build a confident and secure shepherd boy like David. Only the Lord can give them the strength to be a wall, a giant killer, and a man who is able to hear his God every day. This kind of man is one with true masculine strength.

I'm speaking this word to all women, even if you aren't married or have sons. Every man you know is one of His sons. Each of them needs to receive encouragement and affirmation every day in a healthy, godly way from one of God's daughters.

A Masculine Wall #3
"Happy New Year!"

Stephen Hewitt-Brown, 25, was a wall. I'm speaking of him in the past tense because being a wall cost him his life. Hewitt-Brown was on a full elevator going down in his apartment complex in Manhattan. The elevator stopped on the third floor where a woman, Erudi Sanchez, and her 10-year-old nephew started to get on.

As they stepped on, Hewitt-Brown wished the two a Happy New Year. But before the words were even out of his mouth the elevator gave way and began to drop. Instinctively, Hewitt-Brown shoved Sanchez and her nephew back out of the elevator, effectively saving their lives. But the malfunctioning elevator lurched again and Hewitt-Brown became wedged in the gap between the elevator door and the third floor. When the elevator slipped again, Hewitt-Brown was crushed in the gap.[8]

I would love to be able to ask Mr. Hewitt-Brown, "What caused you to act so quickly and so instinctively?" I would like to think his answer would be, "Because it was the right thing to do." I agree with him. It was the right thing to do. It was manly. It was wall-like.

I want to be a man like that. One who will do the right thing when it comes to relating to the women in my world. Most of us will never be called on to make the ultimate sacrifice like Hewitt-Brown did instinctively. But you can still be a wall of protection for those closest to you… especially His daughters.

In his book *Manhood in the Making*, David D. Gilmore states that, "Manhood is the social barrier that societies must erect against entropy, human enemies, the forces of nature, time, and all the human weaknesses that endanger group life."[9]

This quote comes from a social scientist writing from a secular perspective that men are important to every society, vitally important. Men protect. They protect from collapse, attack, and death. They protect from assaults. That's what men do. At least that's what they're supposed to do.

If masculinity is defaced and degraded and the wall of men is torn down, then our culture is left unprotected. We're susceptible of being blown in the direction of the slightest breeze of influence, no matter which way it happens to be blowing at the time. Our children are left uncovered. They're vulnerable to the attacks of the enemy, which is exactly what's happening to our families today. It seems that no one is willing to stand in the gap and protect us. In fact, many choose the easy route, to sit by idly, content to watch as wall after wall tips over and falls down like a row of dominoes.

In his commentary on the violence seen in so many cities as a result of young black men being shot or killed in their altercations with the police, commentator Ken Blackwell said:

> It is right that political and religious leaders, community groups, business organizations, and law enforcement officials are commenting about all the causes and effects of the riots. But one thing seems missing from the discussion, a factor whose omission is unacceptable. It's called fatherhood.
>
> Fatherhood is in crisis all across the country. In 2011, Pew Research evaluated data from the Federal Centers for Disease Control and Prevention's (CDC) "National Survey of Family Growth" and found that "more than one-in-four fathers with children 18 or younger now live apart from their children [pewsocialtrends.org]—with 11 percent living apart from some of their children and 16 percent living apart from all of their children."
>
> Yet among black families, the data are even more troubling. Here are some sobering statistics:
>
> - Nationwide, only 17 percent of African-American children reach 17 in a family with their married biological parents. In Maryland, only 21 percent of black teenagers [downloads.frc.org] reach age 17 in a family with both their biological parents married.
>
> - The 2012 American Community Survey, conducted by the U.S. Census Bureau [cnn.com], found that more than 19 million children across the country—26 percent—are living without a father in the home. In Baltimore, among African-American children, the rate is 69 percent. In an environment in which healthy male role models and, more importantly, caring and capable dads

in the home, simply aren't there, and in which human life is so commonly devalued in neighborhood abortion centers, is it any wonder that cohorts of young men go on rampages when provocation arises?[10]

Question: *Those statistics paint a pretty bleak picture. It's obvious that someone has to do something. It's clear that we need some holy walls in our land. Where are they? Who are they?*

"They were a wall to us."

Chapter 4

As Men Go, So Goes Culture

The first time I remember thinking about men as a wall of protection and security was when I was a brand-new youth pastor at a predominately black church. I saw firsthand the plight of many black single mothers with no husband to help shoulder the load.

I remember one time going to a court hearing for one of my students who had been caught shoplifting. Between cases, my eyes scanned the courtroom. I was stunned at what I saw. Most all the people on trial were young black men while single black mothers filled the gallery. There were almost no older black men in attendance. "Where are the fathers?" I wondered to myself.

This had a profound impact on me. Where were the men? And not just black men. Where were the men of any ethnic background in our schools, our neighborhoods, and churches? It became a lingering question in my mind. It began to dawn on me that there was a real problem here. Men simply were not assuming their rightful place, the place that God had destined them for…protecting others.

I knew in my heart that our children, our wives, our culture were all in desperate need of protection; and it was the men's place to step into that role. In a flash I had a thought that stopped me in my tracks. I had three sons of my own! What was I doing to protect them? What about my wife, my daughter? I knew I had to do something...I just wasn't sure what.

Then one day I came across the following verses in 1 Samuel 25:

> *Yet these men were very good to us. They did not mistreat us, and the whole time we were out in the fields near them nothing was missing. Night and day they were a wall around us the whole time we were herding our sheep near them.*
>
> —1 SAMUEL 25:15–16

I felt myself do a double take. What had I just read? This was a familiar passage that I'd read many times before but this time something was different. Something was tickling the backside of my brain about these verses. What was it? I read the verses again, slower this time. The light bulb flashed on. This group wasn't just any group of guys. Just a few chapters before (1 Samuel 22:2) they seemed to be quite a different bunch. They were in debt, distressed, and despondent. They certainly weren't a wall. These guys could barely stand for themselves, much less stand for someone else. These were David's men before they became known as his "mighty men." This was a ragtag group of four hundred enemies of the state in the middle of a civil war following a leader who was just as scared and confused as they were. They were on the run with their tails between their legs at one moment, then standing strong and protective like a wall not too long afterwards.

So what happened?

What was it that transformed this frightened leader and his men into strong stones who formed a wall of protection around those who were weaker? If we can drill down and identify the cause of their transformation, maybe we can find some clues for a transformation of our own.

If we take a quick peek at the end of 1 Samuel 21, we can see quite a different David than the strong victorious warrior we've come to know. It's easy to picture David as the brave shepherd boy defeating Goliath with just a sling and stone. We remember the story of him standing over the giant's body declaring victory while holding the huge sword in one hand and the giant's head in the other.

But the picture we get at the end of 1 Samuel 21 is very different. In the story, the king of Gath, which is where Goliath was from, recognizes David and threatens to capture him. David, instead of summoning his mighty men and fighting back, he puts on an act. He rants and raves and lets the saliva run down his beard, acting like a madman. The king of Gath was disgusted. He asked his men, "Am I so short of madmen that you have to bring this fellow here to carry on like this in front of me?" (1 Samuel 21:15). He left David to scurry away, still running, still scared.

David was their commander. Saul had put him in charge of an entire battalion of one thousand men. These men had fought alongside him. But now these men were caught in the middle of a civil war between Saul and David, and the battalion was forced to make a choice. They could side with the renegade, the one-time giant killer, or they could side with the current king who was currently hunting David down.

Six hundred men took the easy route and left David to side with Saul. Maybe they were tired of David's leadership. Maybe they were scared of King Saul. Whatever the reason, they gathered their things and took off. So what about the other four hundred men? They made the decision to make their stand with David. Now all they had to do was find him.

They were confused. They thought they knew David. He was not the type to run away from a battle. He actually ran to the battlefield in his face off with the giant Goliath. Now he was running away from Saul and his army. Saul was tall but he was no Goliath. So why would David run? His men knew that David was no coward…so something must be going on. They figured that David must be working on a plan.

But where would he be hiding? They had to find him. If they couldn't find him, Saul would round them up and execute them for treason. Their carcasses would be left out in the field for the birds and the dogs to defame. They knew Saul to be crazy…and he would like nothing more than to make an example of David's renegade army. So where should they search for him?

They knew without a doubt that David would be in the caves, the system of connected caves at Adullam. These caves were large enough for an army to hide in, yet small enough to be easy to disguise. I'll bet they even had a prearranged plan: "If things fall apart, meet at the caves and regroup." Yes, David was having cavetime in the caves at Adullam, and his men would risk their lives to have cavetime with him.

David had been coming to these caves since he was a shepherd boy. He'd been all over this countryside looking for lost sheep, sheep he would usually find hiding in the caves, cooling off in the shade. I'll bet David had even showed his men these caves during their training days. He showed them what great hiding places they were, safe, defensible, with fresh water close by.

Now that David was missing, his men knew they would find him there. They would go and be with him in the caves. They would encourage each other and hear from God. They would rest and train, sharpening their minds and their swords, preparing for the day they would come out and fight. To them cavetime would be a time of preparation for whatever God had for them in the coming months.

The men met with David in the cave at Adullam for a period of time and came out changed. These men were different when they emerged from the cave. They were transformed from a hapless group of thugs and hoodlums, from a torn down, desecrated wall of masculinity, vandalized, attacked, unattended human walls of manhood, into mighty men who were able to stand as a wall of protection. Like the transformation of a caterpillar into a butterfly, these guys were different coming out of the cave than they were going in.

But there are so many hurting people in this world, so many damaged and confused souls crying out for protection. Who do we stand for first? We've seen the overwhelming statistical evidence. The need is so great. Where do we even start?

To me, this is an easy decision. In fact, I don't even have to pray about it. Our first priority is to become a wall for our daughters. I say this, not because I think our sons are not important. But we're supposed to be walls for our ladies first. Why is that? Well, because a woman was the first gift that God gave to Adam. Eve was the first gift to the first man. She was the culmination of all of God's creation, His prized finale, His magnum opus, His creative human crescendo given to Adam. And He charged Adam with the responsibility of standing for her and with her. But what did Adam do? He let her, and all of us, down. But guys, listen to me. We have a chance to redeem Adam's mistake. We have the chance to make it right. We can show up, step up, and honor God by honoring our women.

I am convinced there's no greater call for men today. This is our top priority, to become walls around our daughters: His daughters. Women are being objectified by the media, the porn industry, and out-of-control sex-traffickers around the globe. A wall of protection and security must be built, a rampart must be established, and guys, we're the ones to do it. A new holy wall of godly manhood must be built to surround and protect His daughters, and it's got to be done now, for our daughters, for His daughters, for all women everywhere.

From Lori

How does it make you feel when Jeff and your men speak of being a wall for you?

The first time I heard Jeff speak of a wall of men being built to protect women, I was overcome by several emotions. As I stated earlier, I did not always feel that my husband was being a wall for me. Early on in our marriage, I wasn't mature enough to understand the dynamic going on between us. Today, it's easier to see that, at the time, Jeff simply didn't have the capacity to understand all of the female emotions swirling around in my head. He was busy enough just trying to understand his own emotions and who he was in Christ. Being a wall of protection and security for his family was still an evolving concept for him.

When I first heard Jeff talk about being a wall for me, some of the first emotions I felt at the time were surprise, relief, amazement, gratefulness, and then the desire to understand and embrace this new truth. I may not have fully grasped the concept but I understood that I was safe. Like I said, this was a whole new notion for me. I was still growing in my own identity as a daughter of God.

This may seem a bit odd, but when the men in your home, your church, and your community start to take their places as men of God, things that have been out of order for so long start coming into order. When men begin to walk in the reality of who they are in Christ, it's easier for us women to walk in who we were made to be. When this happened for me, I found a new security and uniqueness, and I felt safe in that. I knew I was gifted, and that gave me a newfound confidence in myself.

I remember at one point in our marriage actually saying to Jeff, "I need you to rescue me." Have you ever felt that way? Have you been able to find the courage to say that to the man in your life? How many of us women just want to be rescued? The call to be a rescuer is to all men, not just to husbands. From creation, men were made to rescue. And it figures that in God's divine design, women were born with the desire to be rescued. Women are born with the deep down need to know that there are godly men covering them and standing as a wall of security and protection on their behalf.

A Masculine Wall #4
"Hit By a Car"

I know I've already used my dad as an example of a wall, but there's another great story about him I've got to tell you. It occurred when I was probably between four and five years old. My sister, Jeni, was three years behind me, making her between one and two. This story took place during the brief time we lived in New Jersey. Our whole family was out one weekend window-shopping when we decided to stop in at the local bakery.

I remember it like it was yesterday even though this probably took place over fifty years ago. It's just one of those stories that has never left me. My parents bought me an amazing cupcake at the bakery that was made in the shape of a frog. To this day, I can close my eyes and see that silly frog. It was covered with gooey, green icing. It had a red tongue and cool bulging eyes that were also made of icing. I remember begging to eat that nasty pastry amphibian, but my parents told me I had to wait until we got into the car. I was upset of course and pouting, thinking maybe I could at least take a lick off the top as soon as my parents looked the other way. I didn't even realize we were crossing the street until Mom held her hand out for me to hold on to. My dad held my sister in his arms, and we stepped off the curb and into the crosswalk. Not only did I not look both ways, I didn't even watch where I was going. All I could think about was taking a big lick of that gross green icing! I was mesmerized by that silly cupcake.

The next thing I knew, I heard a loud screech of tires on pavement and my mom screaming, "*Kirk!*" I looked up just in time to see my dad get hit by a car in the crosswalk. The impact bent him over the hood of the oncoming car but he continued to hold on to his little girl, my sister Jeni. In fact, I could tell that in the heat of the moment, he held onto her even more tightly. He straightened up and by sheer force of will refused to drop to the pavement. I am not sure how fast that car was traveling when it hit my dad, but it was fast enough for the tires to screech when the brakes were applied quickly. The driver, who was a woman, sat there in shock for a second, and then sped away. She was probably just as stunned as the rest of us that my dad was even still standing. There were no witnesses other than us, and the frog of course. Dad calmly led us to the other side of the street. No ambulance or police were called, no emergency trip to the hospital.

I don't remember now if I ever got to eat the frog or not. Needless to say, my dad's act of bravery distracted me from my desire to eat that green icing. From that day forward, I was convinced that my father was indestructible. I thought he might even be some kind of super hero! He was definitely the best dad I knew. I mean really! What other dads could get hit by a car and not go to the ground, crying out in pain? My dad was a wall for his daughter that day. In my mind, there's no better picture of a man standing as a wall of protection than that image of my dad holding on tightly to my little sister even through the impact of the oncoming car. What a great example he was of a wall standing for his family.

Question: *In the same way that my dad protected my sister, what are some ways we can protect His daughters from the things speeding toward them?*

Chapter 5

And He Just Sat There

"Be a wall for your daughters, be a wall for your sons, Heaven come down among us, may Your will be done."[1]

Now the serpent was more crafty than any of the wild animals the LORD God had made. He said to the woman, "Did God really say, 'You must not eat from any tree in the garden'?"

The woman said to the serpent, "We may eat fruit from the trees in the garden, but God did say, 'You must not eat fruit from the tree that is in the middle of the garden, and you must not touch it, or you will die.'"

"You will not certainly die," the serpent said to the woman. "For God knows that when you eat from it your eyes will be opened, and you will be like God, knowing good and evil."

When the woman saw that the fruit of the tree was good for food and pleasing to the eye, and also desirable for gaining wisdom, she took some and ate it. She also gave some to her husband, who was with her, and he ate it. *Then the eyes of both of them were opened, and they realized they were naked; so they sewed fig leaves together and made coverings for themselves.*

Then the man and his wife heard the sound of the LORD God as he was walking in the garden in the cool of the day, and they hid from the LORD God among the trees of the garden. But the LORD God called to the man, "Where are you?"

He answered, "I heard you in the garden, and I was afraid because I was naked; so I hid."

And he said, "Who told you that you were naked? Have you eaten from the tree that I commanded you not to eat from?"

The man said, "The woman you put here with me—she gave me some fruit from the tree, and I ate it."

—GENESIS 3:1–12, EMPHASIS ADDED

In chapter 1 I talked quite a bit about Adam's all-encompassing blunder, but let's take a deeper look at exactly what happened on that fateful day.

What a tragic scenario. A woman is left to fight against a seductive dragon all by herself. And when I say "by herself" I don't mean to imply that she was alone. In fact, if you read closely, you'll realize that she wasn't alone at all; her man was sitting right next to her, watching the whole scenario unfold. In hindsight, this battle could be seen as the most critical battle ever fought in the history of spiritual warfare. This is the one that ended up giving the enemy all the power. Eve, along with her disengaged husband, walked into that battle without even realizing they were in a war.

The dragon began to wear Eve down with his conniving words. Like water dripping on a piece of wood, the serpent eroded Eve's confidence. He tied her in knots until she didn't know what was right and what was wrong. The enemy slithered right into Adam's crosshairs; he was bold enough to mess with his woman right in front of him. It seems to me that the serpent was just begging to be slain. He was a snake to be stomped on with a bull's-eye painted squarely on his foul head. This is a drama yearning for a masculine hero to step up.

But even after this perfect setup, just begging for the hero to enter stage left, there was no response from Adam. No quick, valiant, and decisive masculine action. Nope, Adam just sat there. He sat there on his naked butt and had a snack. He cracked that crisp apple, smacked his lips, and only then did he hear the hissing snicker from that snake.

If you're like me, you know exactly what that accusing snicker sounds like. It's crazy; the enemy tempts us to do it, and then beats us up because we did it! To this day, the enemy is still in our ear, snickering, hissing, and harassing us, pulling us down into failure and self-pity.

> *…she took some and ate it. She also gave some to her husband, who was with her, and he ate it.*
>
> —Genesis 3:6

Over the centuries, Eve has gotten a bad rap. Sure, she's the one who took a bite of the fruit first, but there is no way Adam can wriggle out of this one blameless. He just sat there and watched while his wife was lured into the trap! Are you kidding me? What a wimp he was! There are a few other words that immediately come to mind that I'd like to use to describe his sorry little self, but I don't think they'd make it past the editor. You know what I'm talking about. The same words probably flew to your mind as well! How low down, despicable, cowering, and sissified can a man get? How can a man, the very first man, fail so completely? How is it that he can simply sit by and allow that snake to manipulate his wife and steal the keys to the Kingdom that were rightly his? Or maybe the better question is *why?*

Why did Adam do it? Or more accurately, why did he *not* rise up to protect his wife? Why did Adam do nothing as his wife was violated and manipulated by Satan himself? While the text of Genesis 3:1–12 doesn't explicitly say what happened between Adam, Eve, and Satan, I need to tell you that I know exactly what happened, and why Adam never lifted a finger to protect his wife. And do you want to know how I know? It's not because I have some divine insight and a revelation that no man has ever had before. It's not as if God gave me some kind of technicolor dream depicting the whole scene. Nope. It's not nearly that dramatic. I know why Adam didn't act because I *am* Adam. And so are you. Every mother's son of you, or should I say, every father's son of you.

Read it and weep.

Therefore, just as sin entered the world through one man, and death through sin, and in this way death came to all people, because all sinned.
—ROMANS 5:12

Whether you accept it or not, whether you like it or not, we're all like Adam, and given the same situation we would've screwed up just as badly. On that dark day he wasn't a wall for his wife. And if you're brave enough to admit it to yourself, you've had some dark days in your life when you were no wall for your wife either.

If you're not honest enough to admit it, you're just as weak and gutless as our forefather was. For those of you who understand that we're no different from Adam, it's time to step up. It's up to us, the ones with a clear grasp on reality, to figure out why we're so much like Adam so we can get some much needed help. It's time to turn this thing around! For generations upon generations, men have struggled with the passiveness we've inherited from our earthly father, Adam. But no more! It's time to draw a line in the sand. The buck stops right here! Are you willing to stand with me?

Distraction

Maybe Adam was distracted. Maybe a stone had come loose from somewhere higher up the hillside and was rolling down. Maybe a bird was high up in the tree chirping away on a song. How else could Adam have been close enough to Eve for her to reach over and give him a bite of the forbidden fruit, but not be aware that he and Eve were under a full-on attack? The beautiful snake was bending her ear, and the things he was telling her were captivating.

That's right, I said beautiful. It's my opinion that the serpent was deceptively beautiful and alluring, that is, before he decided to tangle with God's first man and woman. The snake that convinced Eve to eat the fruit bore little resemblance to snakes we see slithering along the ground today. We know this serpent was able to stand and walk and talk, at least until the incident with Eve. After that he was doomed to slink along the ground and hiss. It could be that Adam was simply taken aback by the beauty of this strange being, paying no real attention to what it was saying to his wife.

Or maybe Adam was just sitting there at the breakfast table reading the sports page, zoned out in front of the television, or playing some meaningless game on his iPhone. I don't know how it went down, but it's possible that he was distracted in some form or fashion.

Whatever occurred, however it went down, we do know that Adam wasn't a living, breathing, standing wall for his wife on that day. Living walls stand and protect from outside forces of destruction and evil. They get between their loved ones and the incoming projectiles being launched at them daily, whether those projectiles are physical, verbal, spiritual, or emotional. Living walls make sure that none of the shrapnel is allowed through to cause damage or pain for their beloved.

Have you ever been distracted? Have you ever just tuned out your wife, tuned out your family? Have you ever been so distracted by someone or something that you haven't even paid attention to what is going on in the lives of those closest to you? Have your precious loved ones, the ones you've been put on this planet to protect, been lured, manipulated, molested, and defiled while you were sitting right there at your kitchen table? Dude, for God's sake, for *their* sakes, pay attention!

The dragon tempted and manipulated Eve using his slick words with Adam sitting right there watching the whole thing go down. Satan didn't use a computer; he didn't use media of any kind, but he was effective nonetheless. But today, the enemy has those electronic tools and many more at his disposal. Our families are being battered by an onslaught never before seen in our history. And just like Adam, many men are distracted by images they can't turn away from. The devil doesn't change. Distraction worked on Adam. Distraction works on us too.

ABCNews.com reports that:

> In a recent survey of young Internet users aged 10 to 17, one in five reported they had received unwanted sexual solicitations online, ranging from sexually suggestive comments to strangers asking them to meet them in the real world for sex.
>
> Nationwide, 4,500 cases were reported to police last year in which predators used chat rooms to prey on teenagers. But child advocates

suspect the actual number is much higher, since most incidents are not reported to the authorities.

A profile of a new kind of sexual predator is emerging: one who is technically savvy, targeting girls between 12 and 15—especially vulnerable girls who write openly about their problems.

"Small and lost like me" was one message the Massachusetts girl wrote. She said she wanted to run away from home.

"Unfortunately, the predators can smell a child who is vulnerable, it's like chum to a shark," said Parry Aftab, director of Cyberangels, an Internet safety organization, and author of *The Parent's Guide to Protecting Your Children in Cyberspace*.

The anonymity of the Internet has allowed predators to easily hide or misrepresent themselves. An online friendship can turn into a dangerous personal meeting.

"Every single case that I'm aware of and the FBI is aware of, the children have gone willingly to a meeting," said Aftab. "It's very easy to get a child to go willingly when you understand how vulnerable they are."

"They've become their friends and so they feel very comfortable giving out information they would normally not give out to strangers," said Ruben Rodriguez, director of the exploited child unit of the National Center for Missing and Exploited Children.

After a death in the family, Texas teenager Katy Glover found a friend in a chat room. They talked online for a year, chatting almost every day. Katy was 12 when she first met her friend who said he was 16.

"We kind of like became boyfriend and girlfriend, and eventually, he asked me to take naked pictures of myself," recalled Glover. He sent her a Polaroid camera, and she took some pictures and sent them. When her mother, Shari, found a letter referring to the pictures, she told the friend to stay away but did not contact the police.

"I did think about calling the police," said Shari. "The more I thought about it, the more I thought the police wouldn't know what to do. This was so new…I rationalized that they couldn't do anything."

A year and a half later, Katy and her mother learned from Utah police that the "friend" was actually a middle-aged sexual predator who had been corresponding with a dozen other children as well.[2]

Where are the walls? It's time for men to wake up! Stop sitting there eating a snack while your daughters—His daughters—are lured away and fondled by the devious snake. Be aware! Your home could be under attack right now. Be a wall for God's sake. Be a wall for their sakes.

Fear and Intimidation

Who knows, maybe Adam wasn't distracted at all. Maybe he was simply afraid. We may not like to admit it, but we all get scared from time to time. It's just that it's not usually in the makeup of a man to admit that he's afraid. That admission attacks the very core of who we are and how we were made. If we were made to protect, we also had to be made brave, right?

So Adam may have been scared. Yes, the serpent was beautiful and sleek, but he was also cunning and devious. Adam could tell by looking that this was no ordinary animal. This snake could communicate; he could stand and walk. I can imagine Adam looking at the snake, knowing deep down that something just wasn't right, something was off. He couldn't quite put his finger on it, but something just didn't add up. So Adam did what we so often do. He played it cool. He wasn't going to give the serpent the satisfaction of revealing how scared he really was. He was going to be cool about it. Hey, it's no big deal. In the Garden we talk to snakes every day of the week.

In my own mind, there was a conflict building in Adam's spirit. He knew he should do something, say something, and demand something, but instead he chose to do nothing. He allowed the presence of the beautiful and cunning snake to intimidate him. For the moment, he forgot who he was, the great steward of the Earth, put in the Garden to guard and protect.

It's easy to see that Adam should have mustered his courage, stood to his feet, and stepped between his woman and the snake like a wall. He could've flipped the field from playing defense to playing offense. He could have reared back and taken his best shot. I'm convinced that if Adam could've found the courage to do that one small thing, that God would have rushed to be at his side in an instant.

You see I believe that God was fully aware of what was going on. The serpent wasn't fooling Him. God wanted to see how His kids would handle the situation. God wanted them to call on Him. He was prepared to come to their rescue because it's in His nature to do exactly that. But His kids never called; they never cried out.

Has this happened in your life, in your home? Has this happened with the women God has given you to stand for? Are they being tampered with while you sit by mesmerized by something else or too scared to act? It's time for action. Don't let the enemy intimidate you. Don't let him scare you. Cry out to God. Remember, He is your strong tower, and He's just waiting for you to call out for help. Call out to Him on behalf of the ladies in your life, His daughters. He will show up. He always does.

Deceived and Manipulated

Maybe Adam wasn't distracted at all. Maybe he wasn't scared. Maybe he was simply deceived and manipulated by a brilliant enemy. Yes, Satan has been defeated by the power of the blood of Jesus Christ, but he is still a formidable foe. He knows he's lost the war so he's particularly desperate to take down as many as he can in defeat with him. He's an expert at fighting these battles on battlefields where he knows he holds the advantage, when he can get men to fight in their own strength using their own words.

But Adam didn't even use those weapons. He did nothing…and he said nothing, at least until the enemy spoke. And as this whole situation demonstrates, those are bad tactics. Don't let the enemy even engage you in conversation. Don't give him the opportunity to show his beauty or to give his cunning full run. Don't even let him into your garden! Defeat him before he's ever allowed inside.

I've always wondered about the setup to begin with. Why was the snake there in the first place? How was he able to find himself in an intimate place reserved only for God, Adam, and Eve? You can bet that an uninvited guest at the table of intimacy will always spell trouble. The enemy will win every time if he is allowed to fight by his own rules with weapons he's an expert at using.

It seems pretty clear now but it wasn't so clear to Adam's muddled mind. Uninvited, beautiful, and manipulative guests are dangerous company to keep. Especially when the guests question healthy, godly relationships and boundaries. The serpent called these things into question. He probed them saying, "Did God really say…" (Genesis 3:1) and "You will not certainly die…" (Genesis 3:4). The enemy was, and still is an expert at sowing seeds of doubt in the innocent minds of his victims.

What we can see now, in hindsight, is that Adam shouldn't have stayed there sitting idly on his butt, twiddling his thumbs. He should have jumped up and punched the snake square in the mouth. There's no time to measure political correctness here. Think about that. There's too much at stake. The effects of Adam's decision not to act in that crucial moment have been reverberating down through history. What Adam needed to do was to be a man, to stand up and speak in the face of deception and manipulation.

Let me ask you, how do you respond when pressured with the enemy's relentless words? When he questions God's Word and God's plan for your life and the life of your family, how do you respond? What are you doing when the enemy mocks and calls into question the healthy boundaries God has ordained for your life, His integrity, and His desire for an intimate relationship? Let me ask you something else. Why the heck have you allowed the enemy to have access to your garden, to sit down at your table, and talk with *your* lady?

It's time to consider some very important things here. How is the enemy attacking the women in your life—your wife, your daughters, sisters, or mother? Is he coming after them with temptations, deceptions, withering taunts, and accusations? Are you on your guard, or have you turned away because you've been deceived?

Fatigue

Maybe the reason Adam didn't act was none of those things. Maybe the answer lies in his own humanness, maybe he was just worn out. Adam's job of watching over the garden must have been exhausting. It was a big gig to be sure, tending the garden and interacting with the animals (see Genesis 2:15, 19–20). There was so much to do, so much to care for.

Maybe it wasn't distraction, fear, deceit, or manipulation that kept Adam from rising up. Maybe it was simpler than that. Maybe he was just tired.

I know I get worn out just mowing my lawn, pulling the weeds from the garden, and keeping the garage in order. Adam was given charge of the entire planet! He must have been tired. Maybe he was a little too tired one morning to pay careful attention to Eve and the conversation she was having with the snake. Adam was too tired to stand as a wall and make her safe. It could have been his "too tired" attitude that cost him everything—that ultimately cost us everything.

How about you? Do you feel too tired to stand? Does your lady need you to engage with her? Is she yearning to have meaningful conversation with you? You do realize that it's far better for her to engage with you than with the snakes vying for her attention, right?

Self-absorbed

Maybe Adam was too self-absorbed to stop the snake before he was able to persuade his wife to eat the fruit. Adam had an important job, and that was to spend time with the Creator of the Universe, which made him second in command over the whole Earth. But he was also the number one human on the planet with a smoking hot wife, who was handcrafted by God Himself. Adam was, for all intents and purposes…The Man!

That's pretty powerful and heady stuff. A friend of mine once said the reason his life crashed was that, "he was smoking his own dope." That's *truth!* It's hard to succeed when you're busy getting high on yourself. That might have been what Adam was doing. Maybe he got so high on himself that he was oblivious to what was going on between Eve and the reptile.

Adam may have been too busy looking in the mirror! Can you say "narcissist"? You remember where we get that term, right? It's from the story of Narcissus, one of the great Greek myths. Narcissus was a hunter, who was so handsome that he was tricked by Nemesis into falling in love with his own reflection in a pool. Narcissus eventually drowned because he was unable to look away from his own reflection. Talk about pathetic!

Can you see the parallel here? Are you carried away by your own self-image and self-worth? Are you too busy looking at your reflection to see the conversation your lady is having with a devious reptile? If this is the case, then you've become your own Nemesis…and a knucklehead.

Have you fallen in love with yourself, with your appetites, your aspirations, your desires, your career, your hobbies? As men, it's critical to remember that we were not put here for ourselves, but for Him and for our families. We were put here on this Earth to do His will, by caring for and providing walls of protection and security for those He's put in our care. Why? Because He wants a relationship with them. He wants to live in them and through them, and in order to do that effectively, He needs safe and secure sanctuaries, sanctuaries that you will build for them with God's help. Together with His help, you become a wall of protection for your family. A man and His God working to make sure those inside the walls are safe, free from seducing snakes and deceiving dragons. Of course the problem is, He can't do this if you're too busy looking at yourself.

Clueless

Maybe it was none of those things. Maybe Adam was just clueless. Is it possible that Adam simply didn't recognize the value of the gift God had given him in the person of Eve? Is that why Adam didn't protect her?

It's hard to believe Adam could look at Eve, this stunning beauty, crafted for him by the ultimate Sculptor of human flesh and not want to protect her at all costs. But maybe Adam had been with her so much that he was now taking her for granted, giving the snake an open door to slither through.

I only say this because I've done it myself. I've taken people for granted, people I love and care for most in this world, haven't you? I am embarrassed to say that I've done this countless times to my wife, Lori. Thankfully, I do it less now than I used to, but in the past I was definitely a repeat offender. I was unengaged and clueless, with no excuses.

The problem with being clueless is that the dragon is so devious and such a schemer, he can sense when a woman is unprotected because her man is clueless and unengaged. He's the ultimate opportunist, and he takes this opportunity to insert himself into our lives, sauntering in through the unguarded front door. He slithers his way to the breakfast table and takes a seat. The man of the house pays no attention as the perverted predator fondles his wife, his beautiful, amazing gift from God.

Maybe we'll never know exactly why Adam chose not to stand up for his wife. But the fact remains, he didn't fulfill the role he was put on this earth to fulfill. And it didn't end with Adam. Not standing up as a wall for His daughters is like a cancer that's been passed down the family line… all the way down to you and me. Like the freckle-faced son of a freckle-faced dad, we're a chip off the old block.

Want a couple of examples from Scripture? Let's take Abraham first. On more than one occasion, Abraham didn't act as a wall for his wife, Sarah. In both Genesis chapter 12 and again in chapter 20, in order to save his own skin, he lies about the fact that Sarah was his wife, telling everyone that she was his sister.

And how about Lot, Abraham's nephew? Now here's a weasel for sure. In a story that's hard for someone from a Western culture to believe or even comprehend, Lot offers his daughters to the sexually perverted men of Sodom as they tried to storm into his house and molest the angelic visitors who were inside. (See Genesis 19:1–10.)

And how did Lot choose to sweeten the deal? He told the mob that his precious girls were still virgins! Are you kidding me? What a spineless wuss! How do you think Lot's daughters felt? Imagine their fear as they stood in the background listening to their father offering them up to the mob. I happen to believe that this act of cowardice on Lot's part caused an irreparable breach in his relationship with his daughters. You can read later in chapter 19 of Genesis just how warped their relationship became. Lot's daughters, in another unbelievable turn of events, got Lot drunk, had sex with him, became pregnant and gave birth to sons. These sons were the fathers of two tribes who ultimately became long-time enemies of the Israelites, the Moabites and the Ammonites. These tribes were born out of perversion because Lot failed to stand as a wall for his daughters.

I know. I've been beating up on you quite a bit in this chapter. I've been beating up on both of us. And yeah, I know it stings. That's why I did it. The truth should sting. If it doesn't, you've got more problems than the ones I've outlined here. But never forget, that sting we feel is important because it tells us that we need to make a change. We have to feel, even embrace, the pain of that sting. We have to step up and take responsibility. What Adam failed to do, we must do.

Why didn't Adam or these other guys step up? Who knows? Maybe it's one of the reasons we talked about or maybe I've missed it altogether. Regardless of the reason, we can no longer sit by and allow the women in our lives to be harassed by the enemy. We need to change. And I'm talking about more than just a change in our behavior. I believe we need to be changed from the inside out. Only then can we be made into the wall that God has called us to be. Only then can we stand and protect the women in our lives. We can't make this transformation on our own. We need God's help to be built, rebuilt, and reinforced. We need a Wall Maker to help us.

Are you ready? Are you ready for this inside-out transformation? Are you ready to become a powerful wall of snake-stomping, dragon-destroying masculinity? Then you're ready to turn the page and dive in!

From Lori

What if a woman has no wall to protect her?

Women can't base their identity and security on whether the men in their lives are rising up to be a wall of protection for them or not. As a woman, I know that I can only find my true identity in Jesus Christ and in my relationship with Him. That being said, I can tell you that my security was bolstered as Jeff began to better understand what it meant for him to be a wall for me.

But from the beginning, I always knew that Jesus was my true source, whether I was getting validation from my husband or not. It's a trap that many women fall into, using their husbands as an excuse every time they feel insecure. Your husband can never replace the Savior's place in your life.

God will always be faithful, and He will always be with us. He will provide everything we need for the seasons of life we are passing through. We have to keep our eyes locked on Him.

A Masculine Wall #5
"Use Me"

Ryan Morris likes to say that he's just a "regular guy." Well, if Ryan's a regular guy, then I think we need more regular guys! Ryan was busy pursuing the American Dream, climbing the ladder of corporate success and clicking off all the financial goals on his list. In fact, Ryan told me that there was a time that he believed that providing financial stability for his family was all that was required to be an effective wall. But he learned that being a wall is about a whole lot more. And that's the rest of the story…

You see, Ryan was brave enough to pray one of the most dangerous prayers a man can pray, "Lord, use me." I'm sure Ryan meant those words when he prayed them, but there's no way he could have understood the impact that prayer would have on the life and destiny of his family.

Ryan and his wife, Holly, had been thinking about doing something for God in their spare time, something extra in the evenings and on weekends. They wanted to help a friend of theirs, Kathrine Lee, the founder of the Pure Hope Foundation. Kathrine had transformed a passion to rescue trafficked women into a full-time foundation and ministry. Ryan and Holly shared a dream to become financially independent enough to be able to help Kathrine and her husband, Michael, reach out and rescue His daughters who were trapped in this web of destruction.

And then one day…don't you love that phrase? Just goes to show you that God is powerful enough to change everything in just one day. One day Ryan found himself in his prayer closet, which just happened to be his closet at home. He was praying and staring at a pair of his cowboy boots. In that most unlikely of moments, God answered Ryan's "use me" prayer and planted a calling in Ryan's heart. It was on his knees in his closet staring at those boots that Ryan knew that he was to turn down a lucrative job he'd been offered and move his family to Talco, Texas, to work with Pure Hope.

Ryan emerged from the closet, grabbed Holly and called Kathrine to tell her the news that they were with her. And not just with her in spirit, they really were *with* her. Ryan and Holly turned down a salary, a healthy insurance package, and the stability of a full-time job, and made the decision to move to Talco and help trafficked women in a ministry that hadn't even been born yet. It was time for Pure Hope to make the transition from dream to reality, and Ryan and Holly wanted to be there to help.

Their dream was met with mixed reviews. "Some of our family thought we were crazy and that it made no sense," Ryan said to me.

Within days after the "boot prayer" their home sold, even though it wasn't on the market yet. Meanwhile, Holly's business continued to grow and prosper, and before they knew it they were packing boxes and planning to move their family to Talco and help build Pure Hope. God was providing in ways that were more than the Morrises could have dreamed, and I am glad they did.

Today, Pure Hope is much more than just a dream, it's a reality, and the Morrises are being used by God to make it happen. Trafficked women, once trapped and alone, are being rescued out of darkness and brought into the light. They have a wall of protection provided by their loving Father.

Ryan…a regular guy? Please Lord, give us more regular guys who will get on their knees and pray the prayer, "Use me."

Question: *Will you pray the prayer "Use me" and really mean it? Are you brave enough to pray a prayer that bold? If you are, repeat after me, "God, please use me to be a wall for Your daughters." Okay, now buckle your seatbelt!*

Chapter 6

The Wall of You
Needs to Be Rebuilt

We talked in the last chapter about needing a wall maker to help us make the necessary changes in our lives. God is the original Wall Maker. Out of the dust of the Earth, He breathed life into Adam, the original wall of masculinity. By His own hand He gathered material and formed it into a wall. He blew breath into him and commissioned him "…to work…and take care of" His Garden and all of its contents. (See Genesis 2:15.) The created wall was to stand on the Creator's behalf, but he was never meant to stand alone. Adam was to stand for and stand with a gift, beautiful and unlike any other gift on the planet.

The gift was Eve, the Creator's first daughter. She was taken from the wall but she was not the wall herself. She was never designed to be a wall. She was created second, not because she was less than the first but so she could be covered by the first, protected by the wall, on the behalf of the Wall Maker. The wall and his gift would implement the Maker's great plan. They would establish a rhythm of life that was supposed to make it safe for the two of them and eventually billions of their children. This new planet would become a place for the first family to grow and be protected behind a wall of masculinity that was to insure that these things happened.

But the snake walked through a hole in the wall, an unwatched gate or maybe a broken down or rotted place in the wall. Maybe he had become a trusted friend of Adam's and just went up to the house to get a drink. Regardless of how he did it, he went into the house, sat down at the breakfast table and brought death and destruction by convincing the Wall and the Gift to be disobedient to the Creator's plan. Sin came rushing into the Garden like floodwaters washing through the front door. The attacks of snakes and dragons would now be commonplace in every family, in every house and every land for all of human history. God's initial plan for man to establish dominion and protect His creation was thwarted because the original wall was breached.

The Apostle Paul describes the spiritual, physical, and eternal damage that occurred as a result of the breach in the wall. I touched on this briefly in earlier chapters, but let's take another closer look now. Earlier we read Romans 5:15, but this time I want to add the verses before (12–14) so we can get a broader context not only of how completely the wall was destroyed but also how fully it can be rebuilt, remade through Jesus:

> *Therefore, just as sin entered the world through one man, and death through sin, and in this way death came to all people, because all sinned—*
> *To be sure, sin was in the world before the law was given, but sin is not charged against anyone's account where there is no law. Nevertheless, death reigned from the time of Adam to the time of Moses, even over those who did not sin by breaking a command, as did Adam, who is a pattern of the one to come.*
> *But the gift is not like the trespass. For if the many died by the trespass of the one man, how much more did God's grace and the gift that came by the grace of the one man, Jesus Christ, overflow to the many!*
> —Romans 5:12–15

It was because of Adam's fall, or should I say, his failure, that sin gained entrance and washed right through the wall. Sin flooded into all of humankind like a tsunami, rushing into my life, your life, and the lives of every person ever born. This initial assault was against Adam and his relationship with his Creator and the Creator's daughter, Eve. But the effects of that assault eventually trickle down, affecting all of us. That attack caused massive fault lines to appear in relationships between men and women ever since that day.

I actually had a friend say to me one time that he couldn't wait to get to Heaven so he could hit Adam square in the mouth for letting down his guard like that. While I understand the guy's sentiment, I don't think God would allow that kind of behavior in a place where peace will rule and reign. Not only that, I'm not sure Adam will even be in Heaven. He certainly doesn't deserve to make it. If he hadn't screwed up in such a big way, we would be living happily in the Garden to this day. The big idiot.

But you know what? As soon as I say that I feel the sting of the Holy Spirit's conviction. Neither you nor I deserve to make it either. We're all big idiots just like Adam. Every father's son of us. I believe that you and I would have done the very same thing in that circumstance. It's not a stretch to believe that we could easily read in Genesis about the fall of Jeff, Caleb, Mark, or Jerry on behalf of all mankind. Adam just beat us to the punch...or should I say...the bite.

Genesis chapter 3 describes the aftereffects of the attack in detail:

> Then the man and his wife heard the sound of the LORD God as he was walking in the garden in the cool of the day, and they hid from the LORD God among the trees of the garden. But the LORD God called to the man, "Where are you?"
>
> He answered, "I heard you in the garden, and I was afraid because I was naked; so I hid."
>
> And he said, "Who told you that you were naked? Have you eaten from the tree that I commanded you not to eat from?"
>
> The man said, "The woman you put here with me—she gave me some fruit from the tree, and I ate it."
>
> Then the LORD God said to the woman, "What is this you have done?"
>
> The woman said, "The serpent deceived me, and I ate."
>
> So the LORD God said to the serpent, "Because you have done this,
>
> "Cursed are you above all livestock and all wild animals!
>
> You will crawl on your belly and you will eat dust all the days of your life.

> *And I will put enmity between you and the woman, and between your offspring and hers; he will crush your head, and you will strike his heel."*
>
> *To the woman he said,*
>
> *"I will make your pains in childbearing very severe; with painful labor you will give birth to children.*
>
> *Your desire will be for your husband, and he will rule over you."*
>
> *To Adam he said, "Because you listened to your wife and ate fruit from the tree about which I commanded you, 'You must not eat from it,'*
>
> *"Cursed is the ground because of you; through painful toil you will eat food from it all the days of your life.*
>
> *It will produce thorns and thistles for you, and you will eat the plants of the field.*
>
> *By the sweat of your brow you will eat your food until you return to the ground, since from it you were taken; for dust you are and to dust you will return."*
>
> —GENESIS 3:8–19

I don't know about you, but this doesn't sound like one big happy family to me. It sounds more like many of the families I know, and to be honest, it even sounds like my family from time to time. Can you check off the same negatives I can? Blame, Check! Strife, Check! Hiding, Check! Allowing the curse to rule and reign, Check! And all these things are present because the wall did not do what he was created to do, to protect the gift God gave him, His daughter. Thus, the slithering attack came, tempted, lured, and introduced disobedience into that once perfect place, leaving sin and its destructive aftereffects in its wake.

The Aftereffects

It is my desire that as you read this book you will become aware of the destructive and divisive forces of evil arrayed against you and your people. To think that all of it started because a wall did not rise up and act like a wall. That failure has caused reverberating shock waves to rumble down through the centuries.

So, why don't we just give up? Why should we keep trying? Is there any hope at all?

You bet there is! But in order to understand what kind of hope is needed, we must first get a grip on the aftereffects of the snake's deceptive strategy. Once we're able to get a handle on exactly what happened we can prevent it from happening again, breaking the vicious cycle once and for all.

The First Aftereffect

The very first aftereffect of the attack was the desire to hide from God. Read through the passage again. When Adam and Eve realized they'd sinned, their first impulse was to hide from their Creator. This couple was created to spend time with God and with each other. And if you think about it, because they were created in His image, when they were spending time with each other they were spending time with Him too. During these times, they were one big happy family.

After Adam's failure, they hid from God…in shame. Look at verse 10; they weren't waiting to walk with God through the Garden in the cool of the day, as was their custom. They were busy trying to cover up their nakedness, which was something that had never embarrassed or shamed them before. Disobedience to God and giving in to temptation caused this married couple to hide in shame.

And if you think about it, men and women have been hiding from Him ever since. Sometimes they hide from Him individually and sometimes together as a couple, but hiding from God is what many people do best.

Men hide in many ways and in many places. Often they bury themselves in their work. Their job fulfills their innate desire to be productive even though it will never completely satisfy. That's because men weren't created just for work alone, they were created to work for and with a purpose. Only when a man is willing to give his work to God and pursue the goal of building God's Kingdom is work truly fulfilling. Work was never intended to be a hiding place.

Men hide in their habits too. Habits like watching or playing sports, hunting, drinking, drugs, or hungering after another person's body are just a few of the harmful habits guys can adopt to hide from the Lord. And due to the Internet, running away from the Lord and hiding is as easy as a mouse click or a finger swipe. A flurry of pornographic visions can be delivered to the mind through the very phones we use to speak to our wives and our loved ones. Guys, these are shameful acts, shameful habits, and seductive hiding places.

Here's a bold statement; in my opinion, the forbidden fruit was original porn. I can hear you barking back, "Now hold on just a minute. It was just a piece of fruit…you're taking this too far!"

I wholeheartedly disagree! The fruit was something used to lure Adam and Eve away from their true purpose, which was to have a relationship with God that would draw them to each other. They were to be drawn to each other and driven toward Him. This was the most transparent, honest, naked relationship the world has ever known. It was the forbidden fruit that messed all that up.

The fruit wasn't necessarily bad in and of itself. But, through their disobedience that simple piece of fruit became the focus of their day, their appetites, and their whole relationship. They developed an insatiable desire for the taste of that fruit, fruit that was forbidden for reasons only known to the Creator and the snake. They could have had any other taste the world had to offer but the one taste that they were told to stay away from by their Creator was the one they wanted most of all. It was the taste that would cost them everything, an enticing taste, and one that has left an aftertaste in the mouths of every created being since that day.

The word *pornography* is actually the combination of two Greek words. The first word is *porne,* which means "harlot" and is akin to the word *pernanai*, which means, "to sell."

The second word is *graphein*, which means "to write." In other words, pornography literally means, the writing of harlots. Writing that's written to entice, seduce, steal, and ultimately contaminate. It's easy to think of pornography as something purely sexual. But we miss the fact that the enemy has the ability to use almost anything to seduce us. If all he needs to use is a juicy looking piece of fruit to seduce us, then so be it.

Richard and Linda Sauer, in their article "Pornography: A Distortion of God's Plan," state this powerfully:

"The lie is the same one used in the Garden: Satan is suggesting that God is keeping something good from us. Usually it begins with thoughts somewhat innocent-sounding, such as, 'Women are beautiful; why shouldn't I be able to admire a beautiful woman?' However, porn, like all addictions, tends to progress toward a destructive end from these seemingly 'innocent' beginnings."[1]

Wow! They said it, right there in black and white. The wall crumbled because the forbidden fruit was pornographic. Pornography "tends to progress toward a destructive end…." So what's your porn? What harlot is seducing you with her writing? Come on now, we need to wake up, quit being knuckleheads, and smell the coffee, or the fruit as it were. This isn't a game. There's way too much at stake. The enemy is trying to steal your manhood and assault your "wall-hood." (Yes, that's my new word.)

From Lori
"We've explored some ways that men hide. How about women? How do they hide?"

Like men, women hide too, but in different ways. Many women hide behind their careers. Oftentimes, their work at managing the home and raising kids goes unnoticed, but at work they are rewarded and recognized for their hard work. And not just rewarded with a paycheck but often with a raise in salary, a bonus, or a promotion.

Some women who choose to not work outside of the home use their home as a place to hide. They allow themselves to get wrapped up in all the busyness of raising children, doing all those things that our society says mothers and their children need to be involved in. From homeschooling to soccer clubs to volunteering in the children's ministry at church, women today have no trouble staying busy. And speaking of busyness, I believe busyness provides a very popular hiding place for women.

Women are great multitaskers. We have to be! But that ability can actually work against us. It's our ability to multitask that sometimes tempts us to buy into the lie that we need to stay busy all the time.

Some women hide behind their physical appearance constantly trying to be someone they're not, constantly discontent with who God made them to be, constantly masking.

The Second Aftereffect

The second aftereffect of the attack was a tendency to deflect blame onto someone else. This attack is where a man's habit of blaming his spouse or blaming women in general was born. When God asked Adam about his nakedness and about whether or not they had eaten the forbidden fruit, Adam's response was to play dumb, point to Eve and say, "The woman you put here with me…" (Genesis 3:12).

From that day forward men have been blaming women for their problems. In response, women have been throwing it right back at the guys, and deservedly so. Many of our relationships have devolved into men and women taking turns throwing each other under the bus. In every town, every city, and every nation there are buses running over relationships and destroying the people in them. And the whole time the snake just hisses in laughter.

Come on, man! How spineless can you be? Just like Adam, when faced with your own disobedience, you point to your wife and say, "It's her fault!" When confronted with your own inability or unwillingness to stand as a wall, you gesture toward all women and say, "It's their fault!" When confronted with your failure to follow your God-given purpose, you push it back on God and blame Him for not giving you the right tools or enough money or the right relationships. Blame, blame, blame.

You can take some solace in the fact that you aren't the first guy to blame someone else for your problems, and you certainly won't be the last. Adam did all of the above and I am sorry to say that almost all of the men I know have followed in Adam's footsteps at one time or another. Sorry guys, but I have to say it; it's time to grow a pair! That's right. Get some stones!

It's time to stop blaming your wife. Stop blaming women in general. And stop blaming God for your disobedience. Be a man and own up to your responsibility. Stop blaming everyone else but yourself. Walls don't blame…they stand. So please, repent, apologize, and stand. Stand, stand, and stand some more. And hopefully, once you've made a habit of standing, you'll get used to it and you'll do it no matter what goes on around you.

From Lori
"How do women blame men?"

It's pretty easy for most women to jump on this one because men are so different than women and in many ways, they're the exact opposite (by the way, that's how God designed male and female…to be opposites). Whenever we have something we're not pleased with, we just point a freshly painted fingernail at the closest "he" and blame him.

We blame the men in our lives for doing things or not doing things. We blame them for the way they made us feel or that they haven't paid enough attention to us. We even blame our own bad behavior on our guys. Certainly, there are many times men should do things for us (serve), do things to make us feel better (a note or flowers), to notice us (a timely compliment), or speak a kind word of correction when necessary. But men can't be blamed for all our discomforts, bad moods, bad hair days, and all the other things we may not like.

Another critical key about blaming is not to bring up things from the past that have already been forgiven. Remember, if it's forgiven, it's over. If women continue to beat up their men for sins that occurred in the past, they are effectively tearing down their own wall of protection. Every time we blame or bring back up a sin or misdeed, we're removing a stone from the wall that God has designed to protect us.

The Third Aftereffect

The third aftereffect of the attack was the first curse on the planet. Here are the fateful words from the mouth of the Lord Himself…

> So the LORD God said to the serpent, *"Because you have done this, 'Cursed are you above all livestock and all wild animals!'"*
> —GENESIS 3:14

The curse brought the serpent down…way down. The curse of the Lord brought him down so low that he and all those who sided with him were destined to drop on their bellies and slither in the dust of the Earth.

Remember back in chapter 2 where we read about Jesus bending down and writing in the dirt? I'd like to think that Jesus was taking one more opportunity to remind Satan just how low he and his cohorts were. Jesus would have none of it that day in the middle of that dusty street, just like God would have none of it that day in the Garden described in Genesis 3. God cursed the serpent to eat the dust of the Earth, destined him to have to live on a diet of dirt, mud, and scum. You, my friend, were not created to eat these things. Can you see the picture I'm trying to show here?

Things that are outside God's order and plan for your life may initially look attractive and appealing, but in the end they'll always bring you down. If you choose to live outside God's plan, you are choosing to live a life under the curse. Like the serpent, you'll be destined to slither like a snake through life eating dirt. I hate to admit it but there are many guys who have settled for exactly that, slithering through life eating dirt, living cursed existences. And men who have chosen to live like that can't be walls. Walls don't slither low, they stand tall.

So, what does that look like? Exactly how do men slither and sneak, hide and live in dark reptilian holes? That's easy; let me count the ways. Men drop in the dirt and struggle with anger, shame, sexual sin, greed, hatred, bigotry, pride, rebellion, apathy, human trafficking…you want me to go on? Since the first man chose a cursed life, men all through history have been slithering in the dirt in a million different ways.

The Curse of Objectification

Ever since Adam chose to live a life crawling on his belly like a reptile, we have been cursed to treat each other as objects. We use, manipulate, and abuse others to meet our own selfish needs. In fact, if you think about it, original sin centered around just that, pleasing our own appetites outside of God's plan for us, outside the things He would want for us.

In my opinion, there has never been a time in history where the objectification of others has been worse, especially here in the United States. You can't consider the statistics below and deny the fact that the curse is no longer hidden. It's out in plain sight for all to see.

- There are 300,000 girls in the bondage of sex-trafficking each year in the US (US Dept. of Justice).

- Thirteen is the average age of a girl when she is taken into sex-slavery (US Dept. of Justice).

- Twenty to forty-eight is the average number of times that a girl trapped in sex-slavery is raped every day (Polaris Project, Trafficking NGO).

- Eighty percent of the trafficked girls who are rescued end up back in the sex trade (US Dept. of Justice).

- Seven years is the average life expectancy of a girl once enslaved, objectified, used up and thrown away.[2]

Guys, it's time for us to wake up! This is not why His daughters or His sons were created! This is slithering, sneaking, hiding, failing, and falling. Remember, you can't stand as a wall when you are slithering, sneaking, hiding, failing, and falling. It's time for men to rise up and act like what they were called to be: a *wall!*

From Lori
"How do women slither?"

*W*omen slither just like men. We slither toward some things and away from other things. We slither toward things, such as bad habits, unhealthy relationships, harmful environments, and other things that cause us to live beneath our potential.

We slither away from our potential right into the powerful hold of lies and the trap of the approval of others, worried about what other people think of us. Women too quickly ask, "Do you like this?" or "How does this look on me?" "Do you think I should ____?" "If you were me, what would you do?"

Too often, we fail to realize that we were created to be in a relationship with our Creator, and staying close to Him ensures we're not tempted to slither.

A Ray of Hope

Somewhere deep inside, we all know we've not been created to crawl on our bellies. We know we've been created for more than slithering. That's why we're so quick to blame. It's why we deflect and even lie sometimes. We know what we're supposed to be and we know just how far we've fallen. We know how we're supposed to act, and yet we don't act that way. And that's where we find the fourth aftereffect. And it just happens to be the very first ray of hope in this tragic tale.

The Fourth Aftereffect

If you read the passage, you'll see that right there in the middle of the curse, a ray of hope was born. It's sandwiched right in there between murder and death. It's God's solution to the curse. It's something that only an all-loving, all-knowing, all-seeing and grace-filled God could accomplish.

Can you see it?

It's right there in the last part of verse 15…and it's a baby boy.

> *And I will put enmity between you and the woman, and between your offspring and hers; he will crush your head, and you will strike his heel.*
> —GENESIS 3:15

A baby would be born. God declares that one of Eve's descendants would somehow crush the snake. But to understand what this is really saying, we have to first get a handle on what "enmity" means.

Enmity literally means "murderous intent." God was prophesying that Adam and Eve's disobedience would result in death. Their sin would result in murderous intent leveled by the snake upon every descendant of Adam and Eve. But, there were two prophecies given by God that day. The murderous intent prophecy was just the first one.

God also prophesied that the baby boy, the descendant of Eve, would "crush your head." God is saying that another eternal being would come to Earth and inhabit the womb of another woman. This woman would be the mother of another Adam, an Adam who would go on to establish a whole new race of humanity, a redeemed race.

As you can see, hope was on God's radar from the very beginning. Jesus would be the One who would crush that foul, slithering, dust-eating snake and bring redemption to the children of the first wall who would crumble. The Son of Mary would be the One who would bring hope to the world.

Jesus would come as the new Adam. We learned in chapter 2 that Jesus is referred to as the "second Adam," the One through whom there would be true and eternal hope for all of His sons and daughters. Through Him, the curse would be defeated.

However, in order to crush the snake, the second Adam, Jesus, would have to die. That's what it means when it says, "and you will strike his heel." The snake would bite Him. It had to be that way. To be the kind of wall that would be able to withstand anything and everything that the snake and all of his slithering forces had to bring, Jesus would have to die (get bitten on the heel) and then come back to life. Through His resurrection, Jesus became a new wall of manhood that would rise up, standing victorious on our behalf.

The Apostle Paul explains:

> *For since death came through a man, the resurrection of the dead comes also through a man. For as in Adam all die, so in Christ all will be made alive… "The first man Adam became a living being"; the last Adam, a life-giving spirit. The spiritual did not come first, but the natural, and after that the spiritual. The first man was of the dust of the earth; the second man is of heaven.*
>
> —1 CORINTHIANS 15:21–22, 45–47

As we can see from these verses, Jesus came to counteract the curse. This was a curse that would draw men and women to one another while at the same time, pitting them against each other in a strife-filled, objectifying, manipulating, and dysfunctional love affair.

It is painful even to read this:

> *"Your desire will be for your husband, and he will rule over you." To Adam he said, "Because you listened to your wife and ate fruit from the tree about which I commanded you, 'You must not eat from it,' "Cursed*

81

is the ground because of you; through painful toil you will eat food from it all the days of your life. It will produce thorns and thistles for you, and you will eat the plants of the field. By the sweat of your brow you will eat your food until you return to the ground, since from it you were taken; for dust you are and to dust you will return."

—Genesis 3:16–19

The woman would want the man and not want him. The man would want the woman and not want her. Because of their sin, they were cursed to be severely codependent and have to work very hard for a living. Oh yes, and one more thing; they would ultimately die and become dust. Other than that, things would be great! This is the description of what their cursed existence would be like. It's a familiar existence to us, one that we've all seen repeated far too many times.

Is There Any Hope?

Even though the curse has affected every aspect of our lives, regardless of gender, background, personality, or family history, in the end, God has given us hope.

Through the second Adam, Jesus Christ, God has given us the potential for a restored, or should I say, re-made humanity. Better yet, He's provided for a whole new type of humanity. This is a wall of humanity that's not just an image of God, but God Himself living through His creation of men and women. God has provided a protective wall for all people willing to bow before it, then seek refuge behind it. This new wall is one that the snake can't penetrate or slither under. It's a force that will do more than just stand to protect. It will actually rescue the hurt, forgotten, objectified, trafficked, and lost.

Yes, Jesus is that wall of hope, the new wall. He is the wall who trolls, peeps, and touches differently than the world has ever known. He reaches out to us in a healthy, life-giving way. He's not bent on taking, using, and discarding. All throughout Scripture, in every book of the Bible there are visions, prophecies, and outright signposts pointing to Him. From Genesis all the way through to Revelation the Holy Spirit reveals that Jesus would come as the Messiah, that He would be the Wall for all who would take refuge in Him.

- In **Genesis** He is the offspring who "will crush" the serpent's head.
- In **Exodus** He is the Passover Lamb.
- In **Leviticus** He is the High Priest.
- In **Numbers** He is the water in the desert.
- In **Deuteronomy** He becomes the curse for us.
- In **Joshua** He is the Commander of the Army of the Lord.
- In **Judges** He delivers men from injustice.
- In **Ruth** He is the Kinsman Redeemer.
- In **1 Samuel** He is Prophet, Priest, King, and Wall.
- In **2 Samuel** He is King of grace and love.
- In **1 Kings** He is a Ruler greater than Solomon.
- In **2 Kings** He is the powerful Prophet.
- In **1 Chronicles** He is the Son of David, coming to rule.
- In **2 Chronicles** He is the King who reigns eternally.
- In **Ezra** He is the Priest proclaiming freedom.
- In **Nehemiah** He is the One who repairs the broken down wall.
- In **Esther** He is the Protector for His people.
- In **Job** He is the mediator between God and man.
- In **Psalms** He is our Rock, Fortress, and Hiding Place.
- In **Proverbs** He is Wisdom.
- In **Ecclesiastes** He is the Meaning of Life.
- In **Song of Solomon** He is the Author of faithful love.
- In **Isaiah** He is the Suffering Servant.
- In **Jeremiah** He is the Weeping Messiah.
- In **Lamentations** He assumes God's wrath for mankind.
- In **Ezekiel** He is the Son of Man.
- In **Daniel** He is the fourth Man in the fiery furnace.
- In **Hosea** He is the Faithful Husband.
- In **Joel** He is the One who sends the Holy Spirit.
- In **Amos** He delivers justice to the oppressed.
- In **Obadiah** He judges those who do evil.
- In **Jonah** He is the Greatest Missionary.

- In **Micah** He casts sin into the sea of forgetfulness.
- In **Nahum** He proclaims unimaginable world peace.
- In **Habakkuk** He crushes injustice.
- In **Zephaniah** He is the Warrior who saves.
- In **Haggai** He restores worship.
- In **Zechariah** He is a Messiah pierced for mankind.
- In **Malachi** He is the Son of Righteousness who brings healing.
- In **Matthew** He is the Messiah who is a King.
- In **Mark** He is the Messiah who is a Servant.
- In **Luke** He is the Messiah who is a Deliverer.
- In **John** He is the Messiah who is God in the flesh.
- In **Acts** He is the Spirit who dwells in His people.
- In **Romans** He is the Righteousness of God.
- In **1 Corinthians** He is the Power and Love of God.
- In **2 Corinthians** He is the down payment of what's to come.
- In **Galatians** He is Life.
- In **Ephesians** He is the Unity of the Church.
- In **Philippians** He is the Joy of life.
- In **Colossians** He is the One who holds the Supreme position in all things.
- In **1 Thessalonians** He is Comfort in the last days.
- In **2 Thessalonians** He is the Returning King.
- In **1 Timothy** He is Savior of the worst sinners.
- In **2 Timothy** He is the Leader of leaders.
- In **Titus** He is the Foundation of Truth.
- In **Philemon** He is the Mediator.
- In **Hebrews** He is the High Priest.
- In **James** He is the One who matures faith.
- In **1 Peter** He is Hope in times of suffering.
- In **2 Peter** He guards from false teaching.
- In **1 John** He is the Source of all fellowship.
- In **2 John** He is God in the flesh.
- In **3 John** He is the Source of all truth.
- In **Jude** He protects from stumbling.
- In **Revelation** He is the King of kings, Lord of lords, the alpha and the omega, the beginning and the end!

Jesus Christ took man's place, fulfilling all that which Adam lost, his manhood and his wall-hood. Jesus became the Wall for us all.

As we've seen, the Bible tells us the story of Jesus in every book. The Bible relates how every man and woman has the chance to have a real relationship with the Wall and invite Him to surround them with His protection. They too can become like Him, part of Him. The objectification and manipulation, the slithering and sneaking can stop. Jesus, the new Adam, the second Adam, the very best Adam can totally remake, redo, and revive a healthy relationship between the sexes. Let me assure you that there is hope…and the hope is the Wall named Jesus.

A Masculine Wall #6
"A Wall That Could Swim"

Thank God…some walls can swim. Though you've probably never seen a wall that could swim before, they can, and they can save those who have accidentally fallen in the water. On June 15, 2015, an unnamed woman was rescued by just such a wall after her car plunged off a bridge into the Passaic River in New Jersey. The wall was Jason Moss, an IT Sales Manager who had just come out of the gym and witnessed the woman's vehicle veering off the bridge and into the river. Passersby said that Moss calmly took off his street clothes, put on some gym shorts, and jumped into the water.

He then pried open the door of the vehicle, pulled the unconscious woman out of the car, and delivered her to some waiting emergency responders. When some called him a hero, Moss simply replied, "It was the right thing to do. If I didn't pull her out, she was dead."[3]

> **Question:** *What would you have done if you'd seen a car plunge from a bridge into a river? How does this situation compare to your life? While there may not be women plunging from bridges right in front of you, there may be some who are in other dangerous situations, acting as if they are unconscious. What are some ways you could save them?*

Chapter 7

Five Crucial Wall—
Making Steps

These days we're all looking for shortcuts. We're looking for the easiest and fastest way to get things done. We want fast food, drive through coffee, prepackaged, precut furniture, no-fault divorces, overnight shipping, instant replay, and even groceries delivered to our door.

But the best things in life just take longer. Do you want to learn Spanish? It's going to take a while to become fluent. Do you want to build your own garage or storage shed? Plan on more than a weekend before you're ready to set up shop. Do you want to nurture a strong relationship with your wife? It's going to take more than a couple of bouquets of flowers and a weekend away.

The best things take time, they take focus and intentionality. Let's say you wanted to build a wall along the property line at the back of your yard. Sure, you could probably throw one up in a few hours, sitting on top of the ground and made from lightweight materials. But if you want to build a wall that will last, a wall that your kids and grandkids will still enjoy as they grow old, you're going to have to take the time to do it right.

The same is true of spiritual walls. Walls that are built strong to protect and provide life-giving shelter take time, and they aren't built by amateurs. If you want to be transformed into a wall that can stand guard over His daughters, then you're going to have to submit to the process designed by the Master Wall Builder Himself. This builder is a master craftsman who knows how to build a lasting wall from scratch, using the very best materials. And He builds more than just new walls. This builder has the ability to take old walls, walls that have been defaced and desecrated, walls that are sloping and out of shape, and transform them into sturdy walls that are not only functional to protect, but works of art in their own right, masculine works of art.

Now I'm certainly no master wall builder. I'm not an expert by any stretch of the imagination. However, the Lord taught me a thing or two about building strong walls through an experience I had a few years ago.

Lori and I purchased a house that had a beautiful backyard. In fact, it's one of the features that really drew us to this house in the first place. The yard had a mild slope to it and was peaceful, tranquil, and hospitable. We loved hanging out back there…at least most of the time.

When I say we loved hanging out back there "most of the time," I mean when it wasn't raining really hard. The trouble is, where we live in Oklahoma, when it rains, it often rains very hard, especially in the spring, and this presented a huge problem.

It was on one of those stormy spring days soon after we'd only been in the house a short time that our peaceful backyard was transformed into a not-so-peaceful raging river! This river was so big it had the accompanying small creeks, streams, and other tributaries contributing to the overflow. The rain was coming down in sheets, and as it pooled into rivers of runoff, those rivers raged right through our backyard. The rivers were full of silt, mud, leaves, branches, and…worms!

That's right, worms! We had worms of Old Testament proportions floating right through our backyard, big ones, small ones, wriggly, and squiggly ones. There were worms as thin as your little finger and some as fat as your thumb. Our backyard torrent of water carried all shapes and sizes of those squirmy things.

When I saw the plague of worms, my first thought was, "Well, it could be worse. They could be inside the house instead of out in the yard!" Worms outside I could deal with. But that thought only lasted until I went in my office and discovered that I had a new water feature! One of the bigger tributaries had followed the path of least resistance and flowed right through the back wall of my office carrying with it the cargo of worms.

So picture this. I'm standing in the doorway of my office, in the house we'd just recently moved into, staring at the floor as muddy water poured through the back wall and washed over my shoes. This was muddy water full of squiggly, squirmy, uninvited worms! As any civilized person can tell you, flowing streams full of worms and who knows what else are fine outside but they are definitely not fine flowing through your office! It's funny; the previous owners never mentioned this rather unique water feature in the disclosure statement!

Needless to say, Lori and I were shocked. Living in the new house wasn't supposed to be like this! It was supposed to be fulfilling. It was supposed to be warm and inviting. It was supposed to be…well…dry! But after we recovered from the shock of seeing everything in that office ruined by worms, after we dried everything out and scooped up and threw all the worms outside where they belonged; we came to grips with the fact that we'd purchased a home with a little something extra, an indoor water feature.

So I did what any other mature, upright man of God would do, I got down on my knees and began to pray. I prayed that the previous owners would be blessed beyond measure, blessed with floodwaters all their own, flowing through their bedroom at night, waters brimming with all shapes and sizes of squiggly things much bigger and squishier than the things in my office! "Bless them, Lord!" I cried out. Of course I didn't pray that prayer…but I wanted to! I told you I was a knucklehead!

Instead, it was time to make a plan. I needed to develop a strategy to keep the floodwaters and the squishy worms that came with them outside while keeping the inside warm and dry. Although I wasn't sure exactly what I was going to do about the problem, I did know that it would probably involve building a wall of some kind. And since I'd never done that type of work before, I began to study all kinds of walls and how they're built. I wanted to see what made good walls successful and what caused other walls to tumble over. I learned early on that my new wall would be made from stone. I knew now from experience that a wood wall eventually rots and gives way just like the one currently at the back of my yard.

I studied walls so much I had "walls on the brain." As I would be out and around town, all I could see were walls, especially in my community. There were all kinds of walls, no doubt erected for all kinds of reasons. I spoke with some friends in the landscaping business, and they invited me to observe professional wall builders as they worked at their craft. I was able to see firsthand what the pros did to build a wall that would last. I was like a sponge, soaking up all the intel I could about building strong, sturdy walls that would stand the test of time. I determined that my wall would be built right, designed for the express purpose of keeping floodwaters and squiggly squirmy things out of my house!

In my search to find the best way to build a wall, I discovered five steps that the pros use to build a wall that will last.

Step #1: Observe the Problem Areas

The very first step of building a successful wall was to figure out exactly what was going on. Why did the old wall fail? What was happening when the rain was falling hard? The only way to do that was to observe the backyard while it was raining hard. This was the only way for me to find out what was happening. It would allow me to see where the floodwaters were coming from, and how they were overtaking my existing, rotting, failing wall.

So, the next time it rained, I put on my waders and duck-hunting coat and went outside at the height of the storm and stood in the middle of my backyard as the river began to swell. I'm sure my new neighbors thought I was crazy. I can imagine them rolling their eyes as they watched me out of their windows from the warmth of their own homes. There I was, standing in the middle of my backyard, in a torrential downpour, in a duck hunting outfit. I'm sure I looked as if I were waiting for a flock of mallards to come circling, looking for a place to land. All I was missing was a shotgun! A couple of ducks actually did fly over. They circled the yard…I'm sure there was more than enough water to attract them but they continued on their way. They were probably looking for a place without a guy in waders spoiling the atmosphere!

I stopped watching the ducks and looked down and began to study what was going on down at ground-level. What I saw gave me some valuable information, information I would be able to use when figuring out how to build my wall. I was able to see, in real time during the storm, where most of the water was coming from. Turns out, the water was pouring from my neighbors' yards, from under their fences and then over, under, and through my rotting useless wooden wall, through my backyard, and then into my office.

Being out there in the middle of the yard, in that ridiculous getup, watching the flood helped me to know exactly where the new wall would have to be built. That kind of firsthand knowledge gave me some ideas of how I should build the wall and what materials I was going to have to use. A "wall strategy" was starting to come together in my mind.

While a wall strategy was coming together in my mind, something else was coming together in my spirit…this whole idea of men becoming walls. As I looked across the destruction in my backyard all because of a failed wall, it was easy for me to see the parallel. Our culture is littered with destroyed families, churches falling apart, an eroding moral fiber, all because a wall didn't do its job…just like the wall in my backyard.

Men are supposed to be walls. In these last days, our lives are filled with storms and floods, and I'm not talking about little backyard overflows. I'm talking about tsunamis that wash away whole families. Sometimes these floods slowly rise and spill over their banks causing damage. Other times they just come out of nowhere and bring devastation with them. These floods are financial, relational, physical, spiritual, and emotional. These floods are relentless, pounding at us, showing no mercy. The swells of stress, pain, illness, and disease roll over us like unstoppable waves uncaring and unforgiving.

Are you a wall strong and stable enough to hold back the floodwaters in your life? Or are there gaping holes in the wall that's supposed to be you? Does your wall suffer from holes and rot created over the years by lust, shame, addiction, or maybe just inactivity? Maybe you've grown soft over time. You have a good idea where your holes are, but you're just too lazy to do anything about it. Maybe you've reasoned that it's easier to just sit and do nothing than it would be to rise up, be a man, and take responsibility.

Like Adam, your ancestor, you've given yourself permission to just sit there like a lump through the storms of your life. You're being flooded and swamped from all sides but you don't seem to care. You're content to sit by and watch while the serpent steals, kills, and destroys everything you hold dear.

Well, no more! Today is a brand-new day. It's time to get up off your backside and do something. I challenge you right here, right now to stand up, show up, and take the first step. It's time for you to show up and take a good hard look at exactly what's going on with your wall and why it's not doing what it should be doing. Where is the floodwater pouring through your life? Where are the holes and gaps in your wall? It's time for some hard questions and even harder answers.

Are you ready to get fired up! Are you ready to become the wall that God created you to be? Are you fired up to protect your loved ones from the relentless floodwaters that threaten to pour over their lives every day? Or are you unable to protect them because of the holes in your own wall caused by years of neglect?

Pray and ask God what kind of wall you are. He's the Master Wall Builder and He's faithful to tell you the truth, no matter how tough it might be for you to hear. He will be honest with you and reveal where the holes in your wall are and just how they got there. This is the kind of prayer that should involve much more listening than talking. You're going to have to ask...then shut up and listen to what the Master Wall Builder has to say to you.

I've always tried to have a journal with me so I could write things down as they came to mind. If you are about to hear words from God Himself, don't you think it'd be a good idea to take some notes? Don't put this off for another day. Don't wait for the next flood. Ask God now. He has an opinion...and you know what? He's right! The problem is that we don't usually hang around long enough to listen to what He has to say.

No doubt as you begin to pray and ask God to speak to you, you will hear a variety of voices start to clamor in your mind. Some of the voices will belong to you. Some will belong to the past or to your spouse or your parents. And some voices will come from the very pit of Hell. But if you're faithful to show up and listen, God will come and speak to you, I guarantee it. You'll know it's God because His words will touch something deep inside you. His words will resonate with you in a way no one else's words ever have. You'll just…know. God's voice will light a fire within you. Not a fire that destroys but a fire that ignites a new passion inside you. A passion to rise up and be the man God created you to be, a passion to protect those you love most from the enemy who wants to destroy them. Take some time now and use the lines below to write down the things God is telling you about the kind of wall you are.

_____

_____

_____

_____

_____

_____

Just a reminder, this is not a "one and done" kind of process. In fact, the true value of this exercise is when you get into the habit of doing it often.

Hey, man. It's all about showing up daily, maybe even two or three times a day for two or three weeks in a row. You should be on the lookout for trends in what you're hearing and writing. Is there a theme that most of the thoughts seem to be revolving around? Is there something that keeps coming back? Pay close attention. These themes are like the seeds of God's plan. They are the beginnings of His blueprint to make you into a wall, a flood-stopping wall of masculinity.

Now that you've taken care to observe closely what's going on with the floodwaters coming at you and your family, you're ready to take the next step in the wall building process.

Step #2: Gather Materials and Tools

It's no wonder the wall in my backyard wasn't doing the job. The wall was made from old wooden railroad ties that were probably ancient when they first went in. Now they were mostly rotten and leaning dangerously, ready to fall over in the slightest breeze. The wall desperately needed to be repaired but I didn't want to do all kinds of hard work building a brand-new wall that eventually would just grow old and rot again. I wanted to build a "forever" wall. That meant I needed to give careful consideration to the kind of materials I was going to use. I looked for material that wouldn't rot when water hit it or when dirt filled around it and the earth pushed against it. Then and there, I made the decision to build my wall from stone. It was going to be a rot proof, erosion proof barrier.

I could immediately see that while this might be the right choice, it certainly wasn't the easiest choice. A stack of stones is much heavier and harder to get than a stack of wood. And I was going to need quite a stack of stones to complete this project. I needed enough stones to build a wall that would end up being 20–25 feet long. I needed a lot more stones than I could buy at the lumberyard.

So I called a friend who owns a ranch outside of town. He has more stones than he knows what to do with. In fact, the stones on his land were a nuisance; they made it tougher for him to mow his pastures. He told me I'd be doing him a favor if I hauled off as many stones as I could manage. I started making trips to the ranch with my truck and trailer and any extra helping hands that I could recruit. I hunted down and gathered up stones of all sizes and shapes. I loaded big ones for the bottom of the wall, medium sized ones for the middle portion of the wall, and small stones for the cap.

But I was going to need more than just stones to build this wall. I needed tools as well, tools I didn't have. I had to find picks, shovels, and rakes to dig the trench for the wall and move the dirt away. I needed a chain saw to cut away the old railroad ties and demo the existing wall. Once I got enough stones and all the tools I needed together, I was ready to go to work.

What about you? Have you gathered all the materials and tools that you're going to need to repair and rebuild your wall? Maybe you feel that there has never really been a wall there in the first place. Maybe you've never felt like a wall of manhood. As you read this, you might be feeling that you're going to have to start from scratch. Don't worry about those thoughts. To be honest, I think every man has probably felt like that from time to time, I know I have. In my opinion, if a guy says that he's never felt like that, he's either lying or he just hasn't lived long enough yet. But mark my words…the floods will come.

Just that knowledge alone, that the floodwaters are definitely coming and that you and those you love are in danger of being washed away should snap you to attention pretty quickly. And that's a good thing. When you're aware that something has to be done, you've moved beyond the first step. You've enlisted the help of the Master Wall Builder to help gather your materials and tools and you're ready to take action. Don't take that lightly. Just think about how many guys don't even make it this far!

Okay, now we're ready to gather our thoughts and make a new list. This will be a list of the materials and tools you will need to repair and rebuild your wall. How about a Bible? What about some friends and family members who will be honest with you and help hold you accountable?

What are the other materials and tools that you'll need? Before you just haphazardly jot down a few thoughts, remember, you're not the foreman on this project. God is. And it's always good to get input from the Boss. Ask Him now and take the time to write down some ideas as the Lord brings them to mind.

_____

_____

_____

_____

_____

_____

Now that you and the Master Wall Builder have evaluated your life and discussed where the holes are in the wall (Step One) and you've strategized about specific materials and tools that you will need in the wall building process (Step Two), you are ready for the next step.

Step #3: Remove the Old, Failing, Falling Wall

Now that we've completed the first two steps of the preparation process, we're ready to actually get to work. It's time to roll up our sleeves and pull on the gloves. But we're not ready to build our wall just yet. First, we have to get rid of the old rotting wall. This is a critical step because if we were to try to build the new wall on top of the old, the results would be disastrous. So we have to get rid of the old failing wall first.

In my case, I had to show up in the backyard and begin the difficult, backbreaking task of tearing out and removing the old dilapidated wall. In many places the wood ties were literally disintegrated there was so much rot. In fact, I believe it's fair to say that the wall was really not even a wall at all. It had become dangerous and unreliable on many levels, in many ways. It was leaning badly and ready to fall at any moment. The pick, shovel, and chain saw were my "go-to" tools in this process.

I picked, pulled, kicked, sawed, and dug up the old, rotting, tar-covered railroad ties. Believe me (and Lori!), this job was dirty and smelly! It was hard work, but I knew in my heart that it was the right thing to do. I was dealing directly with the reason for the floods; this old wall was the reason those worms got inside my office. It was hot and sweaty work, but it was incredibly fulfilling. I was filthy dirty, but I was smiling as I loaded up my truck with the crumbled pieces of the old failed wall.

At the end of that process, my back hurt, my arms were scratched, and I had bites all over from the various critters still living in the rotten wood. My clothes were beyond help and needed to be thrown away. But anytime you make the effort to demolish and haul off the old things, you're going to uncover some pretty foul stuff. You're going to get dirty. You're going to be elbow deep in grime. In fact, that's when you know you're doing it right. Whenever you flush out the old, some of it's going to splash back on you. The good thing is that you're getting rid of the old; those things are exposed, evicted, and hauled away.

You see where I'm going with all this, right?

As you survey the scene of the disaster in your own spiritual backyard, what are the things about the old wall that need to be removed? Can you even see evidence that there was ever a wall in place?

Either way, the very first thing to do is to turn to the One who can actually help you in this situation. It's time to ask the Master Wall Builder—God, the Father of Jesus, the One who makes walls out of the lives of men—to come into your life and remove all that is rotten and failing, right this instant.

It might be cliché, but the thing you really need to do right now is to let go and let God take over. You see, the reason the wall is rotted and failing in the first place is probably due to the fact that you tried to build the wall all by yourself. So let's just stop right now before we go on and take care of a little business. To get the wall building process off on the right foot, we have to tear out the old and rotting things first. This has to be done immediately. This process is called repentance. To repent simply means to change your old way of thinking and go in another direction.

Essentially, this means doing away with the old rotting and ineffective way of living your life and taking things "down to the metal," getting a new clean surface on which to build.

I want to encourage you to use the next few lines to write out a prayer to God and ask Him to do this for you:

_____

_____

_____

_____

_____

_____

Congratulations! I'm so proud of you. Not every man has the stones to do what you just did. And you know exactly what I mean. You were man enough to call out to the One who made you a man in the first place. It may have been hard to do, but it was a necessary step in the whole wall building process. I know how it feels, hurtful and helpful at the same time. Digging down and getting all the old stuff out can be a dirty job but the process is cleansing, washing away the filth and replacing it with purity.

That's the way it often is with things like this. There's always a lot of digging, scraping, cleaning, and dumping. But I guarantee that the job you just did, clearing out the old to make way for the new is the most effective thing you could've done at this point of the wall building process. Now you're ready to be rebuilt. But we're still not ready to start on the wall. We have to start deeper, deeper than most folks will ever see. That's what the next step is all about, preparing the ground for the new wall.

Step #4: Pour the Footer

The process of Step Four begins with digging and pouring a solid footing. A footer is defined as "the supporting base or groundwork of a structure." To construct a footing for the wall in my backyard, I dug a trench into the ground along the path where I wanted the new wall to be. To make sure it was as secure as possible, I dug deeper than the previous footer; I had to dig down below where the flooding had occurred. Then I put a layer of gravel in the bottom of the trench and covered the gravel with a layer of cement. Then, while the cement was still wet, I drove rebar steel rods, called "piles" into the footer. This would help insure that the wall would remain connected to the footer. Once the cement hardened, I knew I had a solid and secure foundation on which to start building my new wall. The footer was dug deep into the ground, reinforced with a layer of stone, then of cement and finished off with the steel piles for the wall to tie into. This wall wasn't going anywhere anytime soon. It took a ton of work, digging, pouring, picking, and pounding, but I had gotten rid of the old failing wall and was now prepared to build the brand-new wall in its place.

Once again, you know where I am going with this, right?

If you want your life to be a wall of protection for others, it needs to be constructed on a solid foundation, level and strong. It also needs to be tied into that foundation with immovable piles that go down deep into the trench. Your wall, just like the one in my backyard, will stand or fall, live or die based on how well you prepare this foundation.

Unless your wall is constructed on the firm, steady, and level bedrock of Jesus, you have no hope at all. Floods, disasters, and erosion will pull your wall down, just like the floods pulled down the wall in my backyard. You will lean, rot, crumble and be rendered helpless, useless to anyone seeking protection. Once this happens, there will be no hope for you, your loved ones, your culture, and those who rely on you for protection, covering, and help.

The Foundation, Jesus Himself, said it best in the Book of Matthew, when describing how the foolish and the wise choose to build their walls:

> *"Every one then who hears these words of mine and does them will be like a wise man who built his house upon the rock; and the rain fell, and the floods came, and the winds blew and beat upon that house, but it did not fall, because it had been founded on the rock. And every one who hears these words of mine and does not do them will be like a foolish man who built his house upon the sand; and the rain fell, and the floods came, and the winds blew and beat against that house, and it fell; and great was the fall of it."*
>
> —MATTHEW 7:24–27, RSV

Jesus is our footer, our steady and stable rock. He's our salvation. Unless you're saved by Jesus Christ you have no firm foundation at all. But I can almost hear you say, "Get to the point! How am I supposed to do this? I can't build a wall. I messed up the first time trying to build the old wall all by myself. Why will this be any different?"

That's a great question and here is the straight answer. The key to this new wall building process is making the *iron strong decision* to tie your life directly into the solid rock of Jesus. Remember the steel rebar piles that I spoke of earlier? I drove rebar piles deep into the wet cement. When the cement hardened, those piles became one with the foundation of my new wall.

The steel piles tied into the foundation of your wall are symbolic of the way you are tied to a strong foundation by the iron strong decision to follow Jesus as your Savior and Lord. Those piles tie you into the bedrock, the footing that is Jesus. This foundation is…well…foundational in molding you and forming you into Jesus, making you one with Him. The salvation decision becomes the stabilizing steel rebar in the wall of your life.

I challenge you to take the next few minutes and ask God whether you are tied into Jesus or not. If you haven't, don't wait another second. Storms are on the way whether you're ready or not. And they may be here sooner than you think. Use the lines below to write out a short prayer asking God to tie you into His foundation of Jesus Christ.

This is your iron strong prayer of decision to make Jesus Christ the foundation of your life.

_____

_____

_____

_____

_____

_____

You have now torn out the old wall, set rebar into the foundation, and you are now ready for the next step.

Step #5: Build the Wall

Step Five is the step where you get to build the part of the wall you can actually see. I say that because the clearing away of the old, the dirt prep work, the digging and picking away at the new trench, laying the gravel and cement, driving the piles are all invisible…no one will ever see that part. All the work that you've done up until now will go unseen.

But don't forget, it's the below ground stuff that matters most of all. In fact, whether a wall is secure or not doesn't depend on the wall itself. It depends on whether the wall has a sure foundation. If the foundation isn't properly prepared, the ultimate success of the wall is unsure.

So, this last step called for me to set stones on top of the footer, around the rebar, stacking them in such a way that they leaned into the places that were problems before, places prone to flooding. These were the problem spots that before actually funneled water onto my property. The new wall, made of stone, would be a barrier of flood-stopping material that wouldn't rot or fall down.

The stacking, or fitting, process was like putting together a giant jigsaw puzzle. I had to find stones shaped in such a way that they fit next to or on top of each other naturally. Then, once the stones were set in place, I mixed and then poured a special type of cement mortar between and around each stone. I used my bare hands to work the "mud" to make sure it covered well between all the joints. Eventually the mortar dried, transforming hundreds of individual uniquely shaped stones into a cohesive, single unit. The new wall was made from several different materials and processes into a single secure wall of protection.

The picture of wall building is screaming out at us. There are so many parallels to the walls that God wants to build in this earth. God is passionate about bringing together men from all over who are willing to join together to become a protective wall of manhood for His Kingdom. He wants to tear out the old and rotted walls that aren't working anymore and start over from scratch, building brand-new walls. He wants to dig, stack, form, and then unify.

Just like the stones in my backyard wall gave it form and structure, the good and godly habits you establish over time in your life will allow for stability and strength in your own wall. When you are grounded and tied into the person of Jesus Christ, the habits you put into practice in your life will be like stones that withstand any storm that might come your way…or your family's way.

Take some time right now and honestly evaluate the wall of your life.

Ask yourself what habits and lifestyle choices you need to begin to implement that will tie you into the Foundation: Jesus. I will spend some time in later chapters making a few strong suggestions about what some specific habits might be, but this time is just for you and God, the two of you alone. He's the Master Wall Builder, and it's His opinion that matters most. I want you to get really good at knowing His opinion and hearing His voice.

Help for You

When I first started to rebuild the wall in my backyard, I was overwhelmed. Looking at the destruction and the mess, it seemed like too much for me to tackle alone. It's common to look at the mess we've made in our life and think the same thing. Why bother? It's just too damaged to repair.

But you don't have to fix this by yourself. God never intended for you to be alone through this process, He's already sent a helper to help you do the job right this time. The Helper is the Holy Spirit. He is the one who can see into the future and knows the storms that are heading your way. He knows when they will hit and how you are going to need to prepare for them. He sees these things before they happen, like a weatherman watching the radar can predict when the storm will hit. Jesus describes the Holy Spirit this way,

> *If you love me, keep my commands. And I will ask the Father, and he will give you another advocate to help you and be with you forever— the Spirit of truth. The world cannot accept him, because it neither sees him nor knows him. But you know him, for he lives with you and will be in you. I will not leave you as orphans; I will come to you.*
> —JOHN 14:15–18

And this way,

> *When the Spirit of truth comes, he will guide you into all the truth; for he will not speak on his own authority, but whatever he hears he will speak, and he will declare to you the things that are to come.*
> —JOHN 16:13, RSV

The Holy Spirit is able to see into the future. He knows when the storms will come. He is our defense and our radar.

So, go to Him now in prayer. Then stop talking and listen for a while. Write down the *iron strong habits* that come to your mind, the habits that will tie you in to the foundation of Jesus:

_____

_____

_____

_____

_____

Ask God repeatedly over the next 21 days to help you implement these new habits. Make sure you are doing your part by not just praying. Forming good habits requires action on your part. You need to *do* the things you want to become habits. If you can do that, I promise that on Day 22, you will have pounded strong steel rebar into your life. These habits will tie you in to the foundation of Jesus.

Remember, a firm foundation plus iron strong habits and good lifestyle choices equals a wall of manhood that will continue to stand strong throughout any storm. On the other hand, a slanted foundation plus bad habits equals a slanted and weak wall, which will ultimately crack, erode, and topple over. I don't want to erode or be slanted and weak. I want to be molded and tied in to the foundation Himself.

How about you?

Would It Stand in a Storm?

After several days of tedious, backbreaking work, a whole new wall stood in my backyard. It was a strong, stony, rugged wall—a wall that leaned into the earth, directly against the problem areas.

But would it do its job when the rains came?

I didn't know. It was going to take a storm or two to answer that question.

I am proud to say that when the rains came and the waters roared, not only did the wall hold, but there was no river in my office, nor were there any stinking squiggling worms! The new wall did its job and protected my house. As a wall maker, I had crafted a wall of purpose, and the kind of destruction I'd seen before was averted.

Now when the storms come—and they continue to come—I have nothing to worry about because there is a wall standing in my backyard to keep our home dry and safe. Remember, the wall doesn't prevent the storms, it just keeps you safe when they come.

Do you see the comparisons to your own life?

Do you understand now that we all need a wall maker? As men, we all need someone who will make us into a wall of masculinity for His people. We can't do it alone. Becoming the wall we were destined to be is critically important, especially for our wives and our daughters, because all women are His daughters. He has called men to be a wall for them on HIs behalf.

My wall stands now. What about yours? Is it standing strong or is it leaning or crumbling?

A Masculine Wall #7
"My Mother Is Your Mother"

Near the cross of Jesus stood his mother, his mother's sister, Mary the wife of Clopas, and Mary Magdalene. When Jesus saw his mother there, and the disciple whom he loved standing nearby, he said to her, "Woman, here is your son," and to the disciple, "Here is your mother." From that time on, this disciple took her into his home.

—JOHN 19:25–27

In this passage we are given an insight into Jesus's love for His mother. But the verses hold other interesting cultural clues. Jesus is asking His best friend to follow a manly code that had existed in that culture for millennia. The code was simple, but not easy. This code said that if I die before you do that you will take care of my people.

Look at the last sentence of that passage from the previous Scripture, "From that time on, this disciple took her into his home." John, who was Jesus's closest friend, took the Lord's mom into his home for the rest of her life. He didn't check in on Mary for a couple of weeks when it was convenient. He stood as a wall for her for the rest of her life. He stood on behalf of his brother, his Lord, and for His mom. Wow! What an honor it must have been to serve Jesus in that way.

Many people believe that at the time of Jesus's death, Mary was a widow and that Jesus was her primary caregiver. Now, on the cross, in the midst of all His pain and suffering, Jesus takes care to ensure His mother will be cared for.

So, not only was Jesus a wall, He called "wall-hood" forth out of others as well.

Question: *Both Jesus and John in this passage are demonstrating for us how to be a wall. What are some ways that you can reach out and be a wall for a woman who is widowed or alone? How could you take care of someone's mother on their behalf?*

Chapter 8

Heaven, Coffee, and Walls

I can't wait to get to heaven. While I really have no scriptural basis for it, I feel like there will be forums for us to have individual time with all of the celebrities who live there. Why not? God is relational. He takes pleasure in us getting together in His name. So, why wouldn't He have a time for us to sit and have a cup of heaven's best java with our favorites? And don't you know that heavenly joe is better than anything Starbucks could ever brew! Can you imagine waiting in line to speak with Paul, Peter, and some of the other apostles? My personal apostolic preference is John. I love his Gospel. He was also Jesus's favorite. "...the disciple whom Jesus loved..." (John 13:23). I also love that his name is the same as my favorite cowboy legend, John "Duke" Wayne. And since John was Jesus's favorite disciple, I'd bet you a six-shooter that John Wayne is His favorite cowboy.

But, while there are probably millions, maybe billions of people to connect with on the other side, including the Duke himself, there are two people in particular that I can't wait to see.

The first is totally obvious...the Man...God in flesh Himself...the God-Man...the Wall...Jesus! He is the truest example of wall-hood for all of us. He is the ultimate alpha male. He even called Himself that. "I am the Alpha and the Omega…" (Revelation 22:13). I have gone over our meeting in my mind a thousand times. First of all, I won't mind the wait in line at all. Hey, it's heaven, and we have eternity; it doesn't matter how long I have to wait. I won't be mad or upset; instead I'll be fired up to be there, finally getting to be with Jesus. Here's how it will go down. I will make eye contact with Him just as He is finishing with the person in front of me. I will get on my knees. He will reach for me and stand me up, look me in the eyes, smile, and call my name. He'll call my name with that voice I've never heard with my ears but have heard millions of times with my heart. It's the voice that made me, saved me, and continues to enliven me. He'll speak to me with the voice that doesn't even need the spoken Word in order to communicate. I'm finally in the presence of the One who speaks to me even when He says nothing at all.

"Jeff, it's so good to see you. I've been waiting."

As we make eye contact and He gives me permission with His grin, I will grab Him like I'm never letting go. I'll take a deep breath, smelling Him, experiencing Him with all my senses. I'll laugh and cry…all at the same time. I can't believe I'm actually in His presence, the Lord of my life, just me and Him, grabbing and hugging, laughing and kissing. I'm sure He'll have gathered together my family and friends who have gone before, and the party will explode around us. Being with Jesus is always a party! He's the party who laughs at what the snake tried to do to us unsuccessfully in the Garden. I will finally be standing with my Wall, the One who made me a wall too.

After His security team comes and pries me away from Him and tells me to keep it moving, I know exactly who I'm going to see next: the Lion of War, King David. There have been more books written about David and his successes, his failures, and his powerful poetry than any other Bible character other than Jesus. I'm sure the line to see him will be pretty long too!

Just like I've gone over my meeting with Jesus, I've rehearsed the meeting with the giant-killing shepherd as well. Here's how I believe it will go down. When it's my turn, I will approach as he calls me forward. If he puts his hand out first, I'll put mine out too. If he doesn't extend his hand toward me, I'll proceed carefully. I know this is heaven, but this guy has chopped people's heads off for merely saying the wrong things, so I'll have to mind my Ps and Qs while in his presence. As soon as I am sure that it's safe, I'll look at him and say,

"O, King."

Now at this point, I imagine him raising his hand to stop me. I'm pretty sure he'll quietly correct me, saying something like, "Jeff, there's only one King here, and we all know who He is. Please tell me you've already been to see Him." I'll nod as I inch closer; maybe even hug him if he moves toward me first. While we embrace he'll say, "Ah, I can smell Him on you. His aroma is unmistakable. It reminds me of my shepherding days, fresh, clean wind, mixed with rain on wild grass." He leans in and takes another deep breath. "He smells like frankincense, and myrrh and...yes, even sawdust. My King, the Carpenter, the builder of things. He's a builder of men and a builder of walls too."

I'll take as much time with David as I can. We'll speak of giant slaying, sling swinging, and forging indebted, depressed, and despondent men into walls of masculinity. That's exactly what David did. He took those men who were indebted, distressed, and despondent in 1 Samuel 22:2 and made them into a wall for their people (1 Samuel 25:16). Ultimately these men became such a wall that their exploits are now legendary in all of military history. Killing lions in pits on snowy days, slaying hundreds in just one encounter, wielding swords so tightly that they became part of their anatomy, legends all. These guys were not to be trifled with.

They were protective shields, human safe houses against every element thrown at their people. What a conversation I will have with David about building walls of men, walls of mighty men that is. I want to be a mighty man too, don't you?

The Original Wall

I am convinced that Jesus was David's trainer. Jesus is the One who gave David his power. Jesus, the godly wall, is the One who trained David to be a wall and then trained him to train his mighty men to be walls too.

"How can this be?" you might ask. Jesus was born much later than David. One thousand years later to be exact. So how could Jesus train David when He hadn't even been born yet? Let me explain.

Jesus is eternal God, the ultimate Rock. I believe that when we talk about David, his mighty men, their amazing exploits, and the powerful things they did on behalf of the Lord, we are talking about how their behavior matched the behavior of the Rock, Jesus. Now stay with me here.

When David's men entered the cave in the rock at Adullam (1 Samuel 22:1) to hide with their leader, David, there was much more going on than just a bunch of guys looking for a good hiding place. The Apostle Paul makes it plain for us here:

> *For I do not want you to be ignorant of the fact, brothers and sisters, that our ancestors…all ate the same spiritual food and drank the same spiritual drink; for they drank from the spiritual* Rock *that accompanied them, and that* Rock *was Christ.*
> —1 CORINTHIANS 10:1, 3–4, EMPHASIS ADDED

In the Old Testament, Moses speaks of Jesus…the Rock:

> *How could one man chase a thousand, or two put ten thousand to flight, unless their* Rock *had sold them, unless the* Lord *had given them up? For their rock is not like our* Rock, *as even our enemies concede.*
> —DEUTERONOMY 32:30–31, EMPHASIS ADDED

Again in the Old Testament, Samuel, David's mentor, spoke of Him too:

> *There is no one holy like the* Lord; *there is no one besides you; there is no* Rock *like our God.*
> —1 SAMUEL 2:2, EMPHASIS ADDED

> *The* Lord *is my* Rock, *my fortress and my deliverer.*
> —2 SAMUEL 22:2, EMPHASIS ADDED

> *For who is God besides the* LORD? *And who is the* Rock *except our God?*
> —2 SAMUEL 22:32, EMPHASIS ADDED

The Lord *lives! Praise be to my* Rock! *Exalted be my God, the* Rock, *my Savior!*

—2 Samuel 22:47, emphasis added

David loved the Rock deeply and speaks of Him often:

The Lord *is my* Rock, *my fortress and my deliverer; my God is my* rock, *in whom I take refuge, my shield and the horn of my salvation, my stronghold.*

—Psalm 18:2, emphasis added

For who is God besides the Lord? *And who is the* Rock *except our God?*

—Psalm 18:31, emphasis added

The Lord *lives! Praise be to my* Rock! *Exalted be God my Savior!*

—Psalm 18:46, emphasis added

The Savior is Jesus. And I'm convinced that, by the Spirit, God revealed this to David. He was interacting with the Messiah, Jesus, who was hidden in Him and trained by Him. David knew that he drew his strength and his ability from Him.

May these words of my mouth and this meditation of my heart be pleasing in your sight, Lord, *my* Rock *and my Redeemer.*

—Psalm 19:14, emphasis added

To you, Lord, *I call; you are my* Rock, *do not turn a deaf ear to me. For if you remain silent, I will be like those who go down to the pit.*

—Psalm 28:1, emphasis added

The Lord *is upright; he is my* Rock, *and there is no wickedness in him.*

—Psalm 92:15

But the Lord *has become my fortress, and my God the* rock *in whom I take refuge.*

—Psalm 94:22, emphasis added

Come, let us sing for joy to the LORD; *let us shout aloud to the* Rock *of our salvation.*
—PSALM 95:1, EMPHASIS ADDED

Praise be to the LORD *my* Rock, *who trains my hands for war, my fingers for battle.*
—PSALM 144:1, EMPHASIS ADDED

There can be no doubt that the Rock was, is, and forever will be Jesus. And all men who stand as the wall of warriors that God intended them to be will be standing as He did. We are all chips off the old block, or should I say, chips off the True Rock. In fact, this is what I think Jesus was doing when He changed Peter's name from Simon to Peter. He was revealing this process.

Do you remember? Peter had just answered Jesus's question, "Who do you say I am?" with, "You are the Messiah, Son of the Living God." Jesus is fired up and excited by this. He's so excited that He gives Peter a new name, "Petros" in the Greek, which really means "chip from the rock." Simon was now Peter, a chip from the Rock. Read it for yourself:

Jesus replied, "Blessed are you, Simon son of Jonah, for this was not revealed to you by flesh and blood, but by my Father in heaven. And I tell you that you are Peter, and on this rock I will build my church, and the gates of Hades will not overcome it.
—MATTHEW 16:17–18

Jesus uses the same words here in the New Testament to describe Himself that were used in the Old Testament. I believe He was pointing at His own chest and speaking of Himself when He said,

…and on this rock *I will build my church, and the gates of Hades will not overcome it.*
—MATTHEW 16:18, EMPHASIS ADDED

Jesus is the eternal Rock, and men are His chips. Men are chips or stones that are placed in the Master's sling. We are empowered by Him, the Rock.

We are chips from the Rock. We are connected to one another by the Rock. We are stones from the Rock that will be built into a wall for God in this culture, able to withstand the floods and storms that beat against His people. We are walls, protecting our people, especially His daughters.

There is no doubt in my mind that David would be the first to tell you that it was by the power of Jesus, the Rock, that he was able to train his men. Only because Jesus Himself had empowered and trained him was he able to train others. Jesus and the shepherd boy had spoken many times in the fields as David tended sheep. They practiced slinging together. They rescued lambs from the mouths of lions and bears. Together, they would eventually kill a giant named Goliath. Jesus built him, prepared him, and made him into a wall of manhood. Jesus is a Wall Builder. That's what He does. It was Jesus who made David into a wall.

Now that we have established who built David and his mighty men into a wall to protect their people, I want to look at the wall building process that made them so mighty.

From Lori
"How do you feel knowing you have a wall of men surrounding you?"

I am confident of the team of warriors I have surrounding me, standing as a wall. They are defending me as a woman. I feel safe, supported, encouraged, and capable of being the "me" God created me to be. When I feel this way, I live the hope-filled existence He desires for me to live. Women can freely live as the person they were created to be when they know that there is a protective wall around them. Men can easily become a mighty wall that can't be destroyed when they know what's behind the wall, when they know what they're protecting.

A Masculine Wall #8
"C. S. Was a Wall"

C. S. Lewis was a wall. He was not just an author and famous philosopher, but he was also a friend. He knew what it was to stand and lock shields with a brother. He did so with his friend Paddy Moore during World War I. Lewis made a promise that if Moore were to die in battle that he would care for Moore's mother. Moore ended up dying in battle, and Lewis kept his promise until Moore's mother died in 1951. It was a promise that Lewis kept for over three decades. Lewis made sure that she had excellent accommodations and company for the duration of her life. They became the closest of friends. He stood as a wall for her.

Lewis was also a wall for Joy Davidman Gresham and her sons. Gresham was an avid fan and reader of Lewis's work. She actually traveled to England in 1952 in order to be close to Lewis and have regular conversation with him about his works, especially *The Screwtape Letters* and *The Great Divorce*. She said that these two books were pivotal in her conversion to Christianity. Eventually she moved to London to pursue a writing career of her own, but while she was there her husband abandoned her for another woman. Gresham was alone, the mother of two adolescent boys, with nowhere to go. Lewis stepped in as a wall to care for her and her sons. Around this same time, Gresham was stricken with cancer. In the midst of her battle with cancer, Lewis felt compelled to marry her so that he might legally care for her and her sons. But over time, he fell in love with her and they spent four short, yet wonderfully fulfilling, years together before her death in July of 1960.[1]

I must admit that I am a serious lover of the work of C. S. Lewis and knowing that he was such a wall for His daughter causes me to love him even more.

Questions: *What are some ways that you could help a friend care for the women in his life? Do you have a friend who has a mother who is an invalid, a shut-in, or unable to communicate? Can you set up a time to visit with her? Is there a single mom you know of with children who need care and mentoring? Is there a way you might be able to help them?*

Chapter 9

Get Some Stones,
and Be a Wall

The first step in the wall-building process for David and his men was to escape to the cave. They were being assaulted ferociously, and they knew they needed to go someplace away from the fray where they could get strategic. Their nation was in the midst of a civil war. Things were tough. In fact, there had already been a couple of assassination attempts on David's life by King Saul, who just happened to be David's boss...and father-in-law. Yeah, can you say "awkward"?

So, David was certainly on the run, desperately trying to escape from those who wanted him dead. Needless to say, he was way down on his luck (see 1 Samuel 18–21). But David's men had seen him in action before. They knew he could kill giants and was usually fearless in the face of battle. This kind of behavior wasn't coming from the David they knew. They figured that there must be some strategic reason for David's retreat. They also knew the places he was most likely to hide.

> *David left Gath and escaped to the cave of Adullam. When his brothers and his father's household heard about it, they went down to him there. All those who were in distress or in debt or discontented gathered around him, and he became their commander. About four hundred men were with him.*

From there David went to Mizpah in Moab and said to the king of Moab, "Would you let my father and mother come and stay with you until I learn what God will do for me?"

—1 SAMUEL 22:1–3

When the men arrived at the cave of Adullam they were already warriors, but weren't a wall yet. They were broken, beaten, and scattered. But they showed up. They did something. They made their way to the cave. Yes, they were being assaulted and pursued, but they had the wherewithal to show up where they knew David would be. The whole process starts when you make the effort to show up. These guys had been desecrated, defamed, and derided. They'd been beaten up, spat on, and declared enemies of the state by the government in power. And on top of all that, they were knuckleheads. Sounds kind of like the state of masculinity and the hearts of many men in America today, doesn't it?

But, these men had confidence in David. They knew he would hear from God and get a plan, a man-making, wall-building plan. They needed a plan that would mold them into the epic fighting force known as "David and His Mighty Men." This wall of masculinity eventually made their way out of the cave and made people safe. This was a wall of men who had made the bold decision to be good to people…and good for people.

I am convinced that if men will follow the same process that these men followed, they too will emerge as a mighty wall. David's men knew when they were at their lowest, they needed to learn from their leader. David knew how to make men into walls because the Master had trained him.

Cavetime

Since David and his mighty men honed their legendary process in the cave at Adullam, I call the wall building process "Cavetime." Cavetime is a discipleship growth process designed for guys. It's built around five disciplines or habits that I call, "The Five Stones." I believe that if a man will discipline himself to engage with these stones, he will become a wall. And when he becomes a wall, he will have no time to act like a knucklehead.

I've included a thumbnail version of the Five Stones here. If you'd like to drill down for more detail on the Cavetime process and the discipleship program that accompanies it, I invite you to read my books *Cavetime* and *The Sling*.

Stone #1: Show Up

This is where it all starts. David and his men were under assault and needed a place to hide. They needed to catch their breath and devise a strategy on how to move forward. They could either stay in their distressed condition, beaten down and on the run, or they could make the decision to do something, to get out of the way of oncoming arrows, accusations, and death squads; they could choose to follow their captain into the cave. The cave is a place where they would be able to gather themselves, learn how to use their stones, and emerge from the cave ready for battle.

Jesus did this too. He showed up early (Mark 1:35). He showed up late (Luke 6:12). He showed up often, praying in the wilderness, gardens, mountainsides, people's homes, temples, and weddings. He showed up loud (Hebrews 5:7). He showed up quiet (Matthew 6:6). He was defined, refined, and affirmed by His Father as He showed up to meet with Him when no one else was watching. Sometimes He listened, sometimes He spoke, and sometimes He shouted.

Both Jesus and David honed the ability to show up when no one was watching. These are the places where true character and strength are forged. A man and his God, in private, taking the time for critical training sessions in the dark, both before and after the rattle and prattle of the day. The reason these private training sessions are so critical is so the man can stand when people are watching, when the pressure is on and fickle crowds try to sway them and giants try to defame them. When the enemy brings his worst, the wall will not fall.

David showed up and trained in private so when Goliath came against him and his people in public, the giant had no chance. David showed up so many times in the dark that it was just another day at the office when he had to face the giant in the light of day. When he and the giant were under the lights, show up time became show off time. It was time for

God to show off through David because the two of them had showed up together so many times before in private.

Jesus showed up and trained in private so when Satan tried to destroy Him at the cross in public, He didn't flinch. His habit of showing up in private gave Him the resolve to show up during His very public trial and execution. Private show ups reverberate in public stand ups, not embarrassing screw ups.

Are you showing up? Or do you flinch when the enemy comes against you in public?

Maybe your failure to show up in public is directly related to the fact that you're not showing up with God in private. The enemy has attacked you in the dark places through lust, porn, and private, hidden sin. You're having trouble standing for God in the public places because you haven't been committed to show up in the dark, alone, and private places. But you can change all that. You can make the decision to show up with God in the private times, just you and Him—the two of you.

When men show up, people are safer. When men show up, they become a wall, and lust, porn, and human trafficking are all assaulted in Jesus's name. Personal demons get dealt with and sent to the pit where they belong…right next to Goliath.

Jesus Shows Up in Ireland

My friend Marc is an Irish warrior who now knows how to show up, fight, and stand as a wall. But he wasn't always fighting on the right side. I want him to tell you the story in his own words, in his own way. You can almost imagine his manly voice with a great Irish accent.

> I grew up in a good family in Dublin, Ireland. We were Catholic. I had a kind of textbook understanding of God. He was like an angry grandfather, had a big stick, and was waiting to get me. I went to Mass two or three times a year to relieve my guilt, but God didn't have any real significance in my day-to-day life. I grew up following the crowd. And in Ireland, much of the crowd drinks, and they make it widely available to young children. It's literally part of Irish culture.

So, one day, as the crowd was drinking at a family function, I decided to try some. I was thirteen. For a few years I experimented. By sixteen, I was drinking heavily almost every weekend. At eighteen, I was not only drinking but smoking weed as well. Eventually, I was not just waiting until the weekend, I was engaging in this stuff two to three times a week.

By twenty-one, beer and weed were not enough, so I progressed to whiskey and vodka, as well as experimenting with acid. I was spiraling out of control. Over the next six years, my spiral led me to mixed drinks (whiskey, rum, and vodka) and mixed drugs (smoking hash, taking ecstasy, and snorting cocaine). I was mixing and ingesting anything and everything I could get into my hands, over my lips, and up my nose. Then came the blackouts, losing track of day and time, trouble with the police, and ultimately being arrested for drunk and disorderly conduct. Spending nights in jail became all too familiar.

By the time I turned twenty-seven I had been pulled out of car wrecks, fires, fallen off a 100-foot cliff, had a gun put to my head, fought regularly for fun, jumped out of running taxis, and walked over bridges looking to end my life on more than one occasion. Finally, after a fifteen-year roller coaster of the effects of a life submitted to alcohol, drugs, and the insanity that had become my existence, I found myself depressed, hopeless, and suicidal.

On the heels of a five-day binge, I had come to the end. Driven by constant negative thoughts running through my head, telling me that I was a worthless, hopeless, pathetic piece of garbage, I fell to my knees. As I prepared to take my life, a final fleeting thought floated through my mind. Then that thought began to take shape into these words.

Tears were flowing down my face. My body and spirit were wrenching and wrestling between life and death. Spiritual and physical contortions were taking place. I continued my rant,

"God, if You are real, You'd better do something and help me... *Jesus, I can't live like this! I can't go on. I need You.*"

Exhausted from the frantic, desperate, and heartfelt screams, I fell to the floor and drifted off to sleep. Waking up sometime later, I raised my head. Something was different. The depression I had carried all those years was gone. In fact, I was filled with an unexplainable joy! I felt totally clean…brand new. I wasn't the same Marc who had tried to kill himself. I stood up, rising like a new creation. A few months later I learned in 2 Corinthians 5:17 that's exactly what had happened:

'Therefore, if anyone is in Christ, the new creation has come: The old has gone, the new is here!'

Joy filled me. I had a totally new perspective. I saw myself differently. I saw people differently. Previously they were annoyances at best. Now, they were beautiful works of God's creation. I could see colors, trees, flowers, birds, and nature. Before, everything was bland and gray. I was a self-seeking and unfulfilled wreck. Now, I was without a doubt, *born again!* And I really didn't even know what that meant. Through the work of Jesus, I now felt new, purposeful, vibrant, and alive.

Over the next few years, Jesus would reveal Himself and His plan to me more and more, deeper and deeper. Today I am married to my warrior princess wife, Cynthia. Her presence in my life is truly miraculous. With her, God has blessed me beyond what I deserve and beyond compare. We live in Ireland as missionaries, speaking in churches, teaching in Bible schools, public schools, street corners… anywhere someone will listen to our miraculous story, all throughout Ireland, Europe, and the USA.

I am convinced that when I showed up, Jesus was already there… waiting. He showed up for me in a big way. Much bigger than I could have ever dreamed.

What a powerful example of showing up. When men show up, so does God. In fact, He's already there. He's always ready to take men as they are and make them into walls. Marc's story says to every man that he doesn't have to get cleaned up first in order to be noticed and used. Jesus is just waiting on him to get to the cave. And when he does, Jesus will meet him there. He will speak with him, train him, change him, inform him, renew him, rejuvenate him, and send him out into the world to live a life of purpose—an intentional, living wall of manhood. God does this in the

United States, Ireland, Israel, Zimbabwe, Tanzania, or anywhere else on the planet where men dare to show up.

When will you decide to show up? I challenge you to pull out your calendar and set the time now. Remember, the things that get scheduled get done.

Stone #2: Worship

While showing up gets the process started, it's the second stone, the Stone of Worship, that gets things rolling in the cave. A powerful example of this can be found between David, God, and the men who showed up at Adullam. The intro and first six verses of Psalm 34 read...

> Of David. When he pretended to be insane before Abimelek, who drove him away, and he left.
> *I will extol the Lord at all times; his praise will always be on my lips. I will glory in the Lord; let the afflicted hear and rejoice. Glorify the* LORD *with me; let us exalt his name together. I sought the* LORD, *and he answered me; he delivered me from all my fears. Those who look to him are radiant; their faces are never covered with shame. This poor man called, and the* LORD *heard him; he saved him out of all his troubles.*
> —PSALM 34:1–6

To really appreciate the context of these verses and the power of the stone of worship, you need to know the background of this psalm.

In the "intro" you'll notice that it says it was written when David pretended to be insane before Abimelek. Do you know who Abimelek was? Well, if you don't, you can turn to 1 Samuel 21:10–15 and read the full story, but here's a quick look at the main points.

Abimelek (another name for him was Achish) was actually the King of Gath. Yes, the same Gath where Goliath the giant grew up...way up. Are you starting to see the picture? David had gone back there for some reason, and I think I know why. I think he was trying to drum up some of the old glory. David was feeling down and depressed. It's only natural that he'd try to regain some of that old glory, kind of like trying to fit back into your high school letterman's jacket. David wanted to do something tangible, in the flesh, so he could feel good about himself again. He wanted to feel like he felt when he killed Goliath. His solution was to go to Gath, find another giant, call him out, and kill him. He thought that would make it all better.

Well, that wasn't what happened, was it? The guys in Gath weren't scared at all. In fact, they made fun of him and mocked him. To keep from being killed, David decided to act like he was crazy…embarrassingly so. And it worked. Abimelek thought he really was crazy and let David go. This mighty man of God, this hero, ran away with his tail between his legs acting like a lunatic.

David's life was falling apart. He had gone from being a national hero, a warrior and major player in every aspect of his culture to a scared shell of a man, running for his life. Running to the cave. But he showed up, didn't he? David showed up in the cave, and he worshiped. He worshiped alone in verse 1, "I will extol the LORD at all times…."

Then he worshiped with his band of brothers. Those distressed, indebted, and discontented men who were hiding with him, "…let *us* exalt his name together." He worshiped with spit in his beard and embarrassment trying to shame him. But look what worship does for a man. Check out verse 5, "Those who look to him are radiant; their faces are never covered with shame."

Even though David was running, embarrassed, and hiding, he knew the power of looking to God, allowing Him to deal with his shame through the stone of worship. When we worship, we shift our focus from the darkness of shame and past mistakes to the face of God and the unconditional love we find there. When we worship, we allow God to see all of the ugliness, the spit on our faces, and the dirt in our lives. He literally burns all that away with His fiery radiance. When men worship, God moves in them.

Jesus Worshiped?

Just like David, Jesus was a worshiper too.

That's right. The God-man, the wall of masculinity Himself worshiped the Lord God. That's because men were created to worship. They were created to worship Him with their mouths, their actions, and for that matter, every aspect of their lives. And when they do this, they unleash power and establish a wall of protection. Nothing else on earth can do that. Worship is a powerful part of the wall building process. It brings strength. It bonds and binds men together with their God and with each other.

In the verses Matthew 26:30, Mark 14:26, and Hebrews 2:12 the New Testament writers made sure we knew that Jesus sang songs of worship. What an example for all of us. If Jesus, the God-man Himself needed to worship, how much more do we need to worship?

I get chills when I consider the following. When Jesus led His men in worship at the Passover celebration as recorded in Matthew 26:30 and Mark 14:26, it was probably part of what is known as "The Hallel." The Hallel is the customary finale to the Passover Supper, formally called the "Egyptian Hallel." It was chanted in the temple while the Passover lambs were being slain. How powerful it would have been in that upper room when Jesus, the Passover Lamb, sang the Hallel with His own voice just before going to be slain. The Lamb singing at the top of His voice about the eternal things He was about to do on behalf of all mankind.

Whenever men raise their voices in praise to the Lamb, they commemorate this powerful moment. They summon the power of His voice. Romans 15 gives us a deeper insight about the power of Jesus-led and Jesus-centered worship. It announces that men actually lift their voices with Him when they worship. Together, Jesus and His men worship the Father…

> *May the God who gives endurance and encouragement give you the same attitude of mind toward each other that Christ Jesus had, so that with one mind and one voice you may glorify the God and Father of our Lord Jesus Christ.*
> —ROMANS 15:5–6, EMPHASIS ADDED

When men worship God with "one mind and one voice," Jesus is singing with them. When they raise their voices to God together with Jesus, they become a manly wall of worship.

Worship As a Lifestyle

I have been around a lot of worshipers in my day, but none who live and love to worship more than my youngest son, Cody. Be encouraged by him as you read what Cody has to say about worship...

Worship has been my weapon. The power it has had in my life has taken me through seasons I thought would be unbearable. Ever since I can remember, I have loved to sing. When I was a child, there was nothing more I wanted to do each day than to climb up onto the fireplace and sing all day long with my plastic microphone. Even at such a young age, I remember the freedom and joy I felt as I would sing worship songs loudly in my house, most likely annoying my siblings. The older I got, the more passionate I became about singing and worshiping.

Worship was always on my mind. I dreamed of being on a show like *American Idol* or *The Voice* and singing worship songs. I wanted to glorify the Lord by singing in front of a lot of people. As middle school approached, it became obvious that singing was not the "cool" thing for a guy to do. The cool guys played all the sports. Singing was not seen as a manly thing. I recognized early on that I could believe the lie that singing was not for guys or I could turn that belief around and sing even more. So, given those choices, I decided to sing even more. I sang whenever and wherever I could, in public or private, it didn't matter; I lifted my voice to God.

Through a very oppressive and anxious time in my early teenage years, singing was one of the only things that put me at peace. I would go into my room, shut the door and sing for hours. And I was not just singing, I was worshiping. I could feel anxiety and depression leave. I knew the devil hated it, and that's one of the things I loved most about worship. I knew if I desired my voice to be heard by many, I first had to be consistent in worship when it was just Jesus and me.

As high school approached, I became more and more confident with the gift God had given me. I attended a public school that had a well-known, nationally ranked drama and show choir program. I auditioned using a worship song and was chosen for the top choir. I learned that when a man lifts his voice to God in private and public places, God will bless him in private and public fashion. Our choir earned top honors at national competitions, and I was blessed to be able to sing and perform in Nashville on the stage of the Grand Ol' Opry.

Not long after my high school years, I auditioned for the reality television show, *The Voice*. I won three rounds into the show. While I was not chosen to go to California, the Lord used the process of that show to boost my confidence. I am convinced that private worship sessions between a man and his God is greater than public. I will worship God whenever and however I can.

Cody showed up to worship. David showed up and worshiped. Jesus leads men in worship. Will you show up and raise your masculine voice in worship?

If you will, He will form and fashion you into the wall you were born to become. He will change you and deliver you from your knuckleheaded ways, and you will no doubt become a wall for those around you, especially for His daughters.

Stone #3: Prayer

Prayer engages men in real, transparent conversation with God.

Jesus was a man of prayer, a godly wall of it. Repeatedly in the Gospels He can be seen doing what Mark recounts in the following verse…

> *Very early in the morning, while it was still dark, Jesus got up, left the house and went off to a solitary place, where he prayed.*
> —MARK 1:35

Jesus was intentional about conversing with His Father in cavetime. He was diligent to make time with God, getting His opinion regarding His schedule, His choice of men to be on His team, and where to go next. You need to be having those conversations with God just as Jesus did.

David prayed often. The Psalms are full of his prayers. Here is one of my favorites, especially when it comes to seeking God's help in standing as a wall for His daughters…

> *There will be no breaching of walls, no going into captivity, no cry of distress in our streets. Blessed is the people of whom this is true; blessed is the people whose God is the Lord.*
>
> —PSALM 144:14–15

Like David, you can make a declaration that you are a wall that will not be breached. I know that David was speaking of an actual wall around his city, but I think he may have also had his men in mind when he wrote this. He understood that bricks and mortar were only one type of wall. The most powerful wall will always be the wall of men who stand up for their God. God can build you up as a wall for Himself, as a wall for His daughters. You will be blessed to stand because He is your Lord. Wow! You will be a wall of masculinity if you add this stone to the foundation of your life.

Let's Pray a Wall Building Prayer Together

Because the subject of prayer is broad and multifaceted, I'm going to limit our focus to specific areas that apply to the building and transformation of men into walls. So, I want to limit our prayers to two wall-building questions and one statement. Take the time to write out your answers in the lines provided below. You may even want to start a journal and begin tracking your progress, writing down the issues you are taking to God on a daily basis:

1. Ask God the following question: "Is there anything in my life (habit, way of thinking, unhealthy relationship, sin) that keeps me from standing as a wall for Your daughters?"

_____

_____

_____

_____

_____

_____

2. Ask God: "What steps do I need to take in order to rid myself of the items/issues that I listed in Question #1?"

_____

_____

_____

_____

_____

3. Make this declaration: "In the name of Jesus, with God's help through the power of the Holy Spirit, I am asking to be delivered of (speak the item/issue right here), so I can stand as a wall. I declare that I will be a wall for His daughters. So help me God."

I challenge you to do this during the course of a day, not just once or twice but over and over. If you are flippant about it, don't expect God to be anything but flippant. It's time for you to ramp it up. You've got to step up and show up in prayer day after day, time after time. And when you do, before you know it, you will be a wall. So, are you ready to repeat the above prayer process one hundred times? The guy in our next section was. That's why he was able to change his world.

St. Wall?

The title "Saint" doesn't quite have the meaning it used to. Today it makes me think of some soft religious man or woman with no backbone or conviction, wearing all white and tiptoeing around the tulips like a weakling. "St. Wall" wasn't like that at all. I'm calling him St. Wall because that is what he was…a wall. Patricius, as he was known in his day, was born early in the fourth century A.D. and then kidnapped and sold into slavery while he was still a boy. Does his name ring a bell yet? Maybe you'll recognize him by his other name…St. Patrick.

It's too bad that the day that commemorates him, St. Patrick's Day, is associated with drinking green beer and pinching people. Patrick was a hero in his own right. He was a protective wall for the people of Ireland. He was a Kingdom warrior and fiery praying man of God. In fact, here are his own words regarding his prayer life:

> Tending my flocks was my daily work, and I would pray constantly during the daylight hours. The love of God and the fear of Him surrounded me more and more—and faith grew and the Spirit was roused, so that in one day I would say as many as a hundred prayers and after dark nearly as many again, even while I remained in the woods or on the mountain. I would wake and pray before daybreak—through snow, frost, rain—nor was there any sluggishness in me (such as I experience nowadays) because then the Spirit within me was ardent.[1]

Ardent is defined as "strong enthusiasm." Patrick was strong and enthusiastic about his prayer life. That's why he was able to face some of the most powerful forces of his day. He fought pagan kings and priests. He fought slavery. He faced off with the organized church. He was a fearless wall. And he attributes his stoutheartedness to his wholehearted commitment to prayer.

Patrick prayed what is considered to be one of the most famous prayers in Christian history, "The Breastplate Prayer of St. Patrick." God empowered him as he prayed it, and it was said to have given him powers over pagan kings and demonic forces. While he may not have written the

Breastplate Prayer in its current form, it contains statements and wording that were from his mind and his mouth. I have included the fiery Patrician prayer here for you to read aloud and get a taste of Patrick's passion and heart for God.

> "I arise today
> Through a mighty strength, the invocation of the Trinity, Through belief in the threeness,
> Through confession of the oneness
> Of the Creator of Creation.
> I arise today
> Through the strength of Christ's birth with His baptism, Through the strength of His crucifixion with His burial, Through the strength of His resurrection with His ascension...
>
> I arise today
> Through the strength of Heaven: Light of sun,
> Radiance of moon, Splendor of fire, Speed of lightning, Swiftness of wind, Depth of sea, Stability of earth, Firmness of rock.
>
> I arise today
> Through God's strength to pilot me: God's might to uphold me,
> God's wisdom to guide me,
> God's eye to look after me,
> God's ear to hear me,
> God's Word to speak for me,
> God's hand to guard me,
> God's way to lie before me,
> God's shield to protect me,
> God's host to save me
> From snares of devils,
> From temptations of vices,
> From everyone who shall wish me ill, Afar and near,
> Alone and in multitude.

I summon today all these powers between me and those evils,
Against every cruel merciless power that may oppose my body
and soul.

Against incantations and false prophets,
Against black laws of pagandom,
Against false laws of heretics,
Against craft of idolatry,
Against spells of witches and smiths and wizards,
Against every knowledge that corrupts man's body and soul.

Christ to shield me today
Against poison, against burning,
Against drowning, against wounding,
So that there may come to me abundance of reward.
Christ with me, Christ before me, Christ behind me,
Christ in me, Christ beneath me, Christ above me,
Christ on my right, Christ on my left,
Christ when I lie down, Christ when I sit down, Christ when I
arise, Christ in the heart of every man who thinks of me,
Christ in the mouth of every man who speaks of me,
Christ in every eye that sees me,
Christ in every ear that hears me.

I arise today
Through a mighty strength, the invocation of the Trinity,
Through belief in the threeness,
Through confession of the oneness,
Of the Creator of Creation."[2]

Patrick prayed prayers like these and changed his world. Will you pray
bold, fiery prayers and change your world? If you want to have the results
that Patrick had, then it's time to start the habit of praying a hundred
times a day. Pray a hundred times, and ask God to make you a wall. Ask
Him to show you what the two of you will do on behalf of His daughters…then be obedient to go out and do what He says to do.

Stone #4: The Word

The fourth stone is the Word. The Word is fuel. It's strategic. The Word is ammunition. You have to have the Word in you or you're dead. There is absolutely no way in heaven or hell that you can stand as a wall without living a life constructed according to the blueprint of the Word. Jesus knew this, and He lived by it. Nowhere in the New Testament is this fact more clear than in the following passage:

> The devil said to him, "If you are the Son of God, tell this stone to become bread." Jesus answered, "It is written: 'Man shall not live on bread alone.'" The devil led him up to a high place and showed him in an instant all the kingdoms of the world. And he said to him, "I will give you all their authority and splendor; it has been given to me, and I can give it to anyone I want to. If you worship me, it will all be yours."
>
> Jesus answered, "It is written: 'Worship the Lord your God and serve him only.'" The devil led him to Jerusalem and had him stand on the highest point of the temple. "If you are the Son of God," he said, "throw yourself down from here. For it is written:
>
> "'He will command his angels concerning you to guard you carefully; they will lift you up in their hands, so that you will not strike your foot against a stone.'"
>
> Jesus answered, "It is said: 'Do not put the Lord your God to the test.'"
> When the devil had finished all this tempting, he left him until an opportune time.
>
> —LUKE 4:3–13, EMPHASIS ADDED

The Lord quoted the Word three times in this battle with Satan and the enemy had no response; he could only walk away. Jesus used the Word as an offensive weapon against the scheming logic of darkness. He stood strong and did not crumble. We must follow His example and speak, live, and stand on the truth that is God's Word.

In the same way, David knew that the Word was raw, living, and eternal power. There's no other guide like the Word of God. It is incomparable. David tells us so in the following verses:

Your word is a lamp to my feet and a light to my path. I have sworn an oath and confirmed it, to keep your righteous rules. I am severely afflicted; give me life, O LORD, according to your word! Accept my freewill offerings of praise, O LORD, and teach me your rules. I hold my life in my hand continually, but I do not forget your law. The wicked have laid a snare for me, but I do not stray from your precepts. Your testimonies are my heritage forever, for they are the joy of my heart. I incline my heart to perform your statutes forever, to the end.

—PSALM 119:105–112, ESV, EMPHASIS ADDED

What a beautiful and poetic description. If you intend on being a wall for His daughters, you will need to know what the Word says. You'll need to be so familiar with it that it will inform your choices in matters that seem cloudy in this dark age. You'll need to study it so you won't be trapped. You'll need to memorize it so it jumps out of your mouth before you even have time to think about it. You'll need to let it inform every aspect of your life and being. It has to be your compass and guide; otherwise you'll crash and burn.

Ju Ju and the Word

I have a friend named Pastor Lawrence Peoples. But he used to be known by his street name, "Ju Ju," which stands for Junior. The name alone used to strike fear into the hearts of rival gang members. To this day he carries scars on his face and his torso from his days of running with the gang. He limps because of a bullet still lodged in his ankle. In his own words, he was a "bad, bad man. A thug, addict, and a gangster." And he would do whatever he had to in order to get whatever he wanted.

But he isn't Ju Ju anymore. He's no longer a thug and a gangster. Today he is the senior pastor of a church in Tulsa, Oklahoma, named, "Goin' Hard for Christ." That's right, his church is named, "Goin' Hard for Christ." And that's what he and his members do; they go hard for Jesus. That's because, as Lawrence says, "I used to go hard for the devil, drugs, and gang-bangin'. Why wouldn't I go hard for Jesus? Jesus went hard for me. I can't help but go hard for Him!"

Lawrence loves Jesus passionately. He met Jesus in what he described to me as a "6 x 9". That's a slang term for a prison cell. Lawrence was incarcerated for many years. That's where he and Jesus got to know each other. He met Jesus in a prison cell and fell in love with Him through His Word.

Lawrence told me that he began to "flip the pages" of the Bible and then the "pages began to flip" him. He says the Word of Jesus changed him. He was redefined by it, and now he can't help but devour all he can get of the Word. And when he says the Word set him free, he really means it. That's because in a miraculous set of events Lawrence was pardoned and released by the governor. Yes, Ju Ju is a free man. Not only is Lawrence free to come and go as he pleases physically, he's free in his soul too. And it's all because of the truth of the Word of God. You can read more about Pastor Lawrence and his story as well as access his sermons at his website, www.goinghardforchrist.org.

Stone #5: Community

Without a doubt, it's community that gives the wall its exponential power. Exponential means "rapid growth." And believe you me, you want exponential power, especially at this point in our history. The enemy is increasing his influence in exponential fashion, so we need to pursue exponential Kingdom growth.

Why shouldn't there be an onslaught of men engaged in learning how to use their stones and then "locking shields" with one another on behalf of His daughters? That's how this movement becomes exponential, by learning to lock shields with one another. The locking shields reference is one of my favorites. It comes from the manner in which ancient warriors, especially the Spartans and Romans, used to craft their shields and their battle formations. They would actually lock their shields together in battle. They would stand locked physically with each other to protect each other's blind spots. This formation is called a "phalanx."

This is a powerful image, isn't it? Warriors locked with each other, battling an enemy who is trying to advance against them. This is how we must come together in prayer, like a phalanx. We must do this now!

When men understand the power of standing and locking shields spiritually and physically with other men, darkness is dispelled and the enemy can be defeated. With the power of God in us and the Holy Spirit guiding us in the name of King Jesus, we cannot be defeated!

The reason that the fifth stone is so important and results in such exponential power is due to another concept called "synergy." Synergy means "the whole is greater than the simple sum of its parts." Essentially it means that 1 + 1 + 1 does not equal 3, but rather much more than 3. You've probably seen this at work when you've played with or worked with a team that is really clicking. I know I have.

I'm confident you'll see synergy as you apply the truths found in this book. As we choose to stand together, we will see a synergy that will result in wall after wall being built across our great land in the name of Jesus on behalf of His daughters. By coming together as a community and locking our shields, we will assault sex-trafficking, the porn industry, and all of the evil and darkness that have slithered into the hearts and minds of so many in our nation.

This is what King Solomon, David's son, meant when he wrote this:

> If either of them falls down, one can help the other up. But pity anyone who falls and has no one to help them up. Also, if two lie down together, they will keep warm. But how can one keep warm alone? Though one may be overpowered, two can defend themselves. A cord of three strands is not quickly broken.
>
> —ECCLESIASTES 4:10–12

I am convinced that Solomon watched his father David employ synergistic concepts in battle, and that's what he is referring to in this passage. The language he uses is actually military in nature. He had seen the synergistic and exponential power utilized by David and his mighty men.

Do you see it? It's not found in being alone. It's found in being together in community, reaching for one another. It's found in covering one another. And ultimately, locking shields with two or more brothers so you can see around your blind spots, 360 degrees. That's what the "cord of three strands" means. You are intertwined and interwoven in each other's lives, so much so that together you can see any enemy preparing for an attack, sneaking up and trying to overpower you and your brothers. When you are in community, you are one, and together you can see everything. You can withstand exponentially more together than you can when you're alone. Together, you are synergistic, a group of men and their brothers, woven together by the power of Jesus, unstoppable, synergistic, and exponential.

Jesus knew all about this power. He practiced the fifth stone. One of His first acts after His baptism was to choose His posse of men (see Mark 1:14–20) so that they could lock shields together and preach the Good News. He was always inviting others to be with Him, training them and then sending them out "two by two" in ministry together (Mark 6:7). He didn't send His men out on their own. His goal wasn't to teach them independence. He was instilling in them a sense of community. He wanted teams of men, synergistic walls of manliness. Stone #5 was second nature to Jesus.

Jesus trained His best friend, John, in the exponential power of community. It earned John the title "the disciple whom Jesus loved…" (John 13:23). John is described this way five different times throughout the Gospels. I think it's because he grabbed on to Stone #5 before the other disciples and really locked shields with Jesus. John followed Jesus closely through the darkness of Gethsemane and didn't run away at the trial. John was the only disciple to show his face at the cross. He was the one Jesus would trust with caring for His mother. He was the first man to see the empty tomb. He was also the disciple who lived the longest, probably over 105 years. John not only understood Stone #5, he lived it.

Do you understand Stone #5? Are you locking shields with anyone right now? If not, you should ask God to show you the community you should be locking shields with. Who are the guys who represent your "cord of three strands"? Ask God, and He will show you. Then you can stand up and show up with another brother and watch synergy begin to work exponentially. Together you can be a wall and start standing on behalf of His daughters.

Roper

I hope every one of you finds a Roper. What is a Roper? you ask, It's simple, a Roper is a guy who totally gets and lives Stone #5. David was a Roper, so was his son Solomon. Jesus was a Roper. A Roper isn't a "what," it's a "who."

Steve Roper has been a faithful friend for over twenty-five years. I first met Steve during my youth pastor days. I remember him because of an event that I was planning. It was an event almost everyone else in the city was running away from, everyone but Steve. The ACLU threatened a lawsuit because we were trying to do good in Jesus's name at some local schools. Everyone except Steve Roper and three other men ran like scared little puppies. But Roper stood like a wall.

This crazy guy has stood with me time and time again. He's stood with me every time he's been asked, day or night, regardless of the odds. In fact, recently, he came and stood with me when a group of drug dealers and users were invading the beautiful, quiet little park in our neighborhood. I called and asked him if he would come and stand with me and chase the thugs away. I knew what he would say. In fact, his "yes" was so quick I almost didn't hear it because he was running to his car so fast, while strapping on his gun and grabbing his nightstick. That's just how he rolls. Community is second nature to him. He lives Stone #5, and he has done it so many times he doesn't even have to think about it anymore.

Roper and I didn't have to stand too long against the bad guys. Only a few nights, and just a little bit of yelling and flexing our muscles, letting them know it was our park. We stood as a wall on behalf of our families. The result? Bad guys gone, park safe. That's how real men are supposed to roll.

Do you want a Roper in your life? Look in the mirror! You need to be a Roper! I have found that you tend to attract the kind of person you are. If you're not attracting anyone, look in the mirror first. Go out and find a ministry or group who needs a Roper. I challenge you to start living Stone #5 right now. Find at least one guy you can lock shields with. Then start looking for places to stand as a wall together. You probably won't have to look very far.

A Masculine Wall #9
"St. Wall"

Remember meeting St. Wall earlier in this chapter? His real name is St. Patrick. Not only was he a powerful and fiery prayer warrior, he was the first recorded "abolitionist" in history. That's right, Patrick fought against slavery in a way no one had done before. In fact, he fought against human trafficking that was comparable to what we see today, maybe even worse. Worse, because it was being perpetrated on innocent, newly converted Christian women in Ireland by a British King named Coroticus as the church sat idly by. These girls were being forcibly taken from their homeland while Christian people did nothing to stop the atrocity. But not Patrick. He couldn't sit still and just let it happen. That's because walls like Patrick don't crumple, they stand. Listen to Patrick's own words as he confronts this vile king for his sin and challenges the bishops and other Christian leaders back in Britain to neither accept his tithes, nor eat with him. Patrick was hard-core. He was a wall…

> "Patricide, fratricide! Ravening wolves, eating up the people of the Lord as it were bread…I beseech you earnestly, it is not right to pay court to such men nor to take food and drink in their company, nor is it right to accept their alms, until they by doing strict penance with shedding of tears make amends before God and free the servant of God and the baptized handmaids of Christ for whom He was sacrificed and died…Dogs and sorcerers and murderers, and liars and false swearers…who distribute baptized girls for a price, and that for the sake of a miserable temporal kingdom which truly passes away in a moment like a cloud or smoke that is scattered by the wind."[3]

Patrick pulled no punches. He was a Kingdom warrior who stood as a wall in word and deed, especially for His daughters, daughters who were being stolen and violated. He stood, demanded repentance, and cursed the darkness.

May God help us stand like Patrick! Lord, help us stand against pagan politicians and kings as well as lethargic churches and pastors.

> **Question:** *What can you do in your day to stand as Patrick did in his? Are you willing to pray like he did? Are you willing to stand as he did?*

❧ Section 3 ❧
"Get Strategic"

This section is the presentation of a protective and systematic "wall building" strategy that must take place in the masculine/feminine relationship. Without a strategy, the battle will be lost. No wall can be built without a plan. In this section I will present a simple, straightforward, strategic plan for every man so he can become a wall for His daughters, regardless of age, marital, or parental status.

Chapter 10

Good-bye, Knucklehead

Okay, here's the bottom line; you're going to have to make some decisions. The days of just floating through life taking things as they come are over. It's time to draw a line in the sand and make some strong life-changing decisions. It really just comes down to this: Are you going to continue being a knucklehead or are you ready to make some changes in your life? Next question: Are you willing to change the way you relate to women?

I'm not talking about the way you relate to the few women closest to you or even about all the women you're acquainted with. I'm talking about *all* women, every one of them. Remember, all women are daughters of the Lord, not just some of them. So, whether we're talking about your wife, your daughters, or any woman you might walk past on the street, are you going to continue to objectify them or are you willing to change your attitudes?

I'm serious; this is real. And don't give me any lame excuses like how you're not as bad as some other guys you know. I'm not talking to them. I'm talking to you. We all fall into the trap of thinking, "Well, at least I'm not as bad as that guy over there." Cut that out. You're not in middle school anymore, and I don't have time for weak-minded, spineless attitudes that guys continue to throw in my face any time they're confronted with their sin. Our culture is in a free fall, and we can no longer afford to take a casual approach to this stuff.

143

There's an epidemic in our nation. Yes, that's right. The destructive way that men think about and treat women in this nation, and the rest of the world for that matter, has reached epidemic proportions. It's time for us to act. In earlier chapters, I provided more than enough statistical evidence to prove my point. There are no more excuses. We have a problem, and now's the time to fix it. We need a wall of men. Are you with me?

Hopefully, you're still reading and haven't thrown this book away. So many guys are too weak to change. They either don't finish books that challenge them like this one…or worse, they finish the books but refuse to take the positive steps toward change that will really make a difference in their lives, their families, and their culture.

So if you're faking it…fine. You can go back to your objectifying ways or you can just sit there, refusing to change, content with being part of the problem instead of part of the answer. But I'm going to ask you to do one thing. Get out of our way because the rest of us are moving forward, and we don't need to be tripping over your lazy rear end.

For those who are still with me, it's time to get strategic. I'm going to challenge you to make *three strategic decisions*. I'm confident that if you can find the courage to stand up, show up, and make these decisions, you'll start a process that will transform you into a stone—a stone that will be a critical part of a growing, expanding *Wall for His Daughters*.

Strategic Decision #1:
Treat Women the Way Jesus Treated Them

The first strategic decision you must make is to decide to treat women as Jesus treated them. Earlier in the book, we took a close look at the way Jesus treated women. There were certain things He never did…things that too often we find ourselves doing. These are the things I want to focus on in this first strategic decision.

Stop Trolling

You must learn to troll differently. Remember, Jesus didn't troll like other men. Most men have fallen into a trap of trolling for women's bodies. They don't know how to deny their flesh so they end up trolling with their eyes, then their hands, and in some cases their entire bodies.

But Jesus wasn't like that at all. He trolled for women's souls, not their bodies. We need to be a wall of men who will troll for the souls of women and understand that all women are daughters of the Father. All women deserve respect, honor, and protection. They need to be kept safe. We need to step into our destiny and become a wall of masculine safety for them.

Please pray this prayer with me:

> Jesus, please help me to stop trolling the way I have been. Help me stop trolling on the Internet. Help me stop trolling at the office, at school, when I drive, and even when I sleep. Deliver me from my trolling ways. Deliver me from objectifying women. Please help me see all women as Your daughters. In Your mighty name I pray. So be it.

Stop Peeping

Second, you must stop peeping. Remember, Jesus didn't use women as a means to an end. He didn't set them up in compromising situations for His own pleasure. He didn't look at them or listen to them for a cheap thrill. He didn't get some kind of sick pleasure from catching them in a compromising situation. Jesus was all about making women safe, especially those who had been compromised in some way. He was strong, safe, and clean. He was a wall for them, stepping into the gap, shielding them from those who wanted to take advantage of them. He didn't use women, period. He protected them and redeemed them, and set them free to live better lives.

Please pray this prayer with me:

> Jesus, please help me to stop peeping like I have been. I want to stop looking at women for cheap thrills. I want to see all women the way You see them. I want to be strong, safe, and pure in my body and my mind toward all women. Please help me see women as Your daughters. In Your mighty name I pray. So be it.

Touch Like He Touched

Third, you need to touch women as Jesus did. He touched them with a pure heart, and when they touched Him, their hearts were made pure. Since Jesus saw them as His daughters, women to be treated with love, respect, and dignity, He didn't allow touching to degenerate into something cheap or inappropriate. We must not touch His daughters inappropriately and, unless they are our wives, we should never touch them sexually. We must be vigilant and always committed to appropriate and healthy touch.

Please pray this prayer with me:

> Jesus, please help me to touch women the way You did. Help me touch women with respect, dignity, honor, and purity of heart and mind. Please help me refrain from touching women I have no business touching. Help me refrain from allowing my mind to linger with thoughts of touching women inappropriately. I want to touch women the way You touched them. I pray that You would be able to touch Your daughters through me. Thank You, Jesus, it's in Your mighty name I pray. So be it.

Strategic Decision #2

Now that you've prepared your heart and your spirit by asking Jesus to help you treat women the way He did, you're ready for the next challenge. First, I want you to go back and reread chapter 7. Remember, that was the chapter where we discussed the *Five Crucial Wall Building Steps*. Can you remember all of them? Have you taken those steps yet? Go back to chapter 7 and find those steps. Write them down here as a prayer list for you to focus on:

Step #1 _____

Step #2 _____

Step #3 _____

Step #4 _____

Step #5 _____

Please pray this prayer with me:

> Jesus, I humbly ask for You to build me up. I want to be the man
> You want me to be. I want my life to be built on the foundation of
> You and nothing else. I thank You that You have taken out the old,
> rotted, and crumbling wall and have reconstructed a new one in its
> place. I am now a wall...founded on You. I will not crumble. In Your
> mighty name I pray. So be it.

Strategic Decision #3

The third and final strategic decision you must make is a commitment
to establish Cavetime in your life. This will insure that you'll be able to
endure as a strong wall for years to come. This isn't complicated. Make the
simple decision to practice the five stones of Cavetime starting today. Do
you remember the five stones we talked about in the last chapter? Write
them down below.

Stone #1 _____

Stone #2 _____

Stone #3 _____

Stone #4 _____

Stone #5 _____

Please pray this prayer with me:

> Jesus, I am asking You to help me live the five stones of Cavetime. I
> want to be a man with stones. I want to treat women like You treat
> them. I want to be a wall. Please, Lord, I don't want to be a knuck-
> lehead. I know You're consistent. Help me with my inconsistency.
> Please help me practice Cavetime daily, weekly, monthly, and yearly
> for the rest of my life. I pray this in Your mighty name. So be it.

I have no doubt that if you make these strong strategic decisions and pray through them, then pray through them again and again, (remember the example set by St. Wall?) that you will become a wall for His daughters. And once you become a wall, you will be ready to join the movement. You'll be locking shields with other guys like me, guys like Steve Roper, Ryan Morris, and thousands of other men who can no longer just sit idly by doing nothing.

Chapter 11

Create Electronic Walls

"Planned electronic walls on the nation's borderlines will use the latest surveillance, sensor, and communications tools. But can technology alone take the place of sturdy physical barriers?…As construction gets underway, observers wonder if technology—even the most advanced surveillance tools available—can substitute for physical barriers and vigilant Border Patrol officers."[1]

In the quote above from his article entitled "Building a Virtual Wall to Protect Our Borders," John Edwards refers to technologies being tested for the purpose of building a type of "cyber wall" to protect the United States from terrorists invading our borders. He outlines some pretty amazing stuff. But in the end, he concludes that actual "physical barriers" and "border patrol officers" need to work in conjunction with technology to get maximum protection and impact. In his view, electronic walls are not enough.

What I want you to realize is that spiritually speaking, it's the very same way. You are that "physical barrier" and "border patrol officer" for your people. I love that word picture. I've talked a lot in this book about becoming a wall and his description is exactly what I'm talking about—a barrier that stands against any terrorist or predator—protecting those you are responsible for.

But as important as that is, I also think it's important to be aware of the times you live in. You need to be in touch with the times your people live in, especially your daughters. I spoke earlier about how the serpent is the ultimate terrorist and predator and how he will try and slither his way into your homes and into the lives of all who live there. He is seductive, and he uses every means he can to access your people and then objectify them. You need to patrol the borders of your home and watch over the ones who live there, especially His daughters.

That's why I believe that you must be electronically strategic and savvy when it comes to protecting the borders of your home. Do you know what *savvy* means? It means "experienced, knowledgeable, well-informed, and shrewd." Bottom line? If you are savvy, no one is going to sneak up on you. When you are a savvy masculine physical barrier, you won't be the kind of guy who gets taken advantage of. You won't be caught sitting idly at the table with a slithering snake lying to your wife and stealing your daughters.

So, you've got to stop using the excuse that technology is just "too confusing" or "too advanced," or "just for the younger generation." You can't say this and you can't think this way either. You can't simply crumple and allow the snake to slither in electronically. I am going to suggest that you, as the physical barrier, the border patrol officer, consider establishing the following electronic walls in your home and in your life. If you are serious about being a wall, you will do this. If you are serious about protecting His daughters, you will do this now!

For You

This whole process starts with you. You're the one who has to show up first. The wall is useless when the foundation is compromised, cracked, and crumpling. So, after making the strategic decisions I outlined in chapter 10, take these bold steps to establish electronic walls in your home, especially in your own personal life:

#1: All of your personal devices (phones, computers, tablets, etc.) must have blockers installed on them.

First of all, you need a blocker, which is an electronic wall installed to filter out the slithering, nasty, pornographic things that can be easily accessed, both intentionally and unintentionally. If you don't do this, it would be like taking all this time and effort to build a wall, then busting a gaping hole in it. By not taking this step, you're inviting the snake to slither in and have his way in your mind, your spirit, and eventually your body. I guarantee it. And the brutal truth is that after he has kicked your butt, he has an open door to go after your people. You must be the first to get victory and stand tall in this area. You've got to lead the way in wall building.

Here are three suggested blockers and one excellent article to assist you as you stand…

- **American Family Online**: afo.net
- **Covenant Eyes**: covenanteyes.com
- **X3 Watch.com:** x3watch.com
- **Focus on the Family**: You can find a great article on this topic on the Focus on the Family web site.[2]

Note: *Don't use the excuse that these applications cost too much.* Yes, they will cost you something, but how much is your purity worth? How much is it worth to you to be clean in your mind, body, and spirit?

Many of you spend a ton of money every month on things like cable, Netflix, pay-per-view, and other subscription services. You somehow find a way to pay for those things…right? Well, I challenge you with this question: Are those things worth more to you than your purity? Are they worth more than your relationship with your wife and kids? Come on, man, stop making excuses! Find the money, and invest in some electronic walls. It's time for you to stand up and be a wall.

#2: You must allow for all personal access codes to be set by someone you trust deeply, someone you can't easily convince to give them to you.

This is a pivotal step. You must have someone you can lock shields with and trust deeply with these things. With each of the apps I mentioned, the first step is to establish an access code. The whole idea of the blocker of course is for you not to have this code…but someone you trust will have it. Believe me, you're not as strong alone as you are when you are part of a three-fold cord. If you think you are strong enough to handle the access codes all by yourself, then it's only a matter of time before the snake will talk you into bypassing or disabling the blockers all together. You need someone to stand with on this.

Trust me on this one. I've done it. In fact, almost every guy I've worked with has done it. In a weak moment we come under attack, and we end up using the code to disable the blocker. That's why you've got to have someone who will stand strong with you on this one, someone who will never give you the codes. It's for your own protection and the protection of those who are depending on you to be a wall for them.

#3: Download these apps.

In addition to the electronic walls established by the blockers, you'll need some shields, some electronic shields that you can lock up with as well. These shields are aggressive applications that will regularly send out Bible verses and articles to you in order to build you up and encourage you. They will also put you in touch with other guys across the world who are fighting this same battle…and winning.

There are two apps I highly recommend. They're both free and available in the Apple iTunes store.

- **Cavetime Giant Slayers**
- **Man Up God's Way**

Note: But these are only two. If these don't seem like a good fit, that's fine. But find something that connects with you and where you are. For more ideas on great apps that will help in the battle read "The 5 Best Apps Available for Christian Men."[3]

Now that you've set up electronic walls for yourself, it's time to consider what you'll need to do in order to protect His daughters from electronic attack.

For His Daughters

Do you remember this scripture?

> *Yet the men were very good to us, and we suffered no harm, and we did not miss anything when we were in the fields, as long as we went with them. They were a wall to us both by night and by day, all the while we were with them keeping the sheep.*
>
> —1 Samuel 25:15–16, ESV

This was the report about David and his mighty men after they had been having Cavetime. These guys had become a manly safe place for the people of the region. They were a wall of protection. They were vigilant, awake, and aware both day and night.

What would be said about you?

Are you awake and aware?

Are you a safe place?

Are you watching while they sleep?

Are you watching while they are awake?

Do you notice what's happening in their lives…especially what's happening to your daughters electronically?

I know this sounds kind of weird, but stay with me.

I want to make two suggestions to you as you stand as an electronically savvy physical barrier for your daughters…

Suggestion #1: Know what your daughter (His daughter) is watching on television, on her phone, on her computer, etc.…

I can almost hear you saying, "But it's her phone, her computer, her iPad…."

My response to this is pretty simple. The way I see it, if you're paying the bill and if she's living under your roof…she's your responsibility to protect. She may think those things are hers, but they are actually yours.

They belong to you, and you are letting her use them. I know that response is old school and isn't the most politically correct attitude to have. I know a ton of dads who would never want to take that bold of a step, realizing that they'll probably upset their daughter and be seen as overbearing and controlling. Controlling? Heck yeah, it's controlling! It's controlling something that can be very harmful to your precious daughter.

Never forget this, my friend. *You are called to be a father first and a friend second.* Fatherhood and friendship are two aspects of your relationship that will sometimes line up and sometimes won't. That's just the way it is. Friends may come and go, but fathers protect first; that's their natural inclination. Fathers also realize that protecting and covering are ways to show how much dads love their daughters.

I encourage you to put the same blockers on any of your family members' electronics that are on yours. This will establish a mutual accountability and shield of safety. Your people will also respect you for applying the same rules to yourself as you're applying to them. With the blockers I suggested earlier, you will get a report of sites accessed by the people using your devices and alerted in the case of any suspicious sites. Remember, you are the border patrol agent. This is your job.

Finally, you should be aware of what she is watching and who she is conversing with on Facebook, Snapchat, Instagram, YouTube, Vimeo, and any other vehicles through which the enemy might use to get to her. If you don't know what some of these applications are, do a little homework to find out. All it takes is a quick Google search to learn all you need to know. I promise you that your daughters are using these tools on their computers and smart phones right now. But stay vigilant. What is popular tends to change almost every month, and you will need to stay on top of the trends. The enemy is an opportunist…just waiting for the tiniest crack in the wall.

Please remember some of the examples I provided for you earlier in the book of predatory men who slithered into the lives of unsuspecting daughters using these types of lures. You are her first line of defense. If you crumple, she is at risk. You are that physical barrier for her protection.

Suggestion #2: Know who your daughter is chatting/texting/speaking with electronically.

The first step is to just be observant. By watching, listening, and paying careful attention you can usually follow this suggestion pretty easily. It's my opinion that if you're covering her in prayer, the Holy Spirit will alert you to the things you need to be aware of. He will guide you and help you protect her. So pray for your daughter often, and then open your eyes to what is going on in her life. Spend time with her. Let her know how much you care. Be inquisitive.

The second step in following this suggestion is to simply ask her who she's been texting or connecting with lately on Facebook, Snapchat, or Instagram. Have her show you. If all of the texting or other social media history have been erased, that's a giant red flag. You should raise an eyebrow and ask why the history was erased.

In fact, you should probably get your own Facebook, Snapchat, and Instagram accounts so you can monitor her account. Let her know that the reason you're doing this isn't because you don't trust her, it's because you care. You should always work very hard to show her that you love her deeply and you're committed to protecting her and staying involved in her life. This will usually help her accept what she might see at first as an intrusion into her life. But remember, you're not trying to be her friend. You're her father.

Now that we have established a general strategy for building your personal wall and for becoming a protective wall for your daughters, I want to get into some specifics for those of you who are married.

Chapter 12

If You're Married

...but woman is the glory of man.

—1 Corinthians 11:7b, esv

If you're married, you should memorize the verse at the top of this page. It's really just the last seven words of 1 Corinthians 11:7, but for all of us married guys, those words are important to remember, so true and so telling. What do I mean by this? I mean that when I see your wife, I can tell a whole lot about you, my brother. If she's tired, beaten down, lacking vision, dumpy, haggard, and ready to fold at any given moment, it could be that you're failing as a husband. Or maybe it's the opposite, she's not beaten down at all; she's trolling and putting it all out there for other men and the whole world to see in public, on social media, or anywhere else someone might notice her. Either way, it could be an indication that you're failing as a wall for her.

Now I'm not saying that she can't have a bad day now and then, or even a bad week, a bad season, or that there may not be an exception to my rule from time to time. But when a married woman has a dark cloud over her head or when she's out looking for affirmation from other men, odds are that you're not taking care of business. Now, if your wife fits one of my descriptions, you may be upset at me about now and ready to chuck this book out the window, flush it down the toilet, or burn it. But wait a minute! Just hear me out and let me finish my thought before you start flushing.

I want you to see and understand the power and potential that resides in the relationship you have with your wife. You can't just blow this off. Your relationship with her is the second most important force in your life. The first, of course, is Jesus. But the second is your wife. Why? Because she belongs to someone; she is someone's daughter…God's daughter. She's His girl. She's His gift to you. And in my not so humble opinion, when the King and Creator of the Universe has crafted a handmade gift just for you, you should open it, and protect it, and treat it with the utmost of care.

That's what the Apostle Paul is speaking about in the verse we started the chapter with. Let's look at the whole verse in context…

> *For a man ought not to cover his head, since he is the image and* glory *of God, but woman is the* glory *of man. For man was not made from woman, but woman from man.*
> —1 CORINTHIANS 11:7–8, ESV

The context of these verses is actually a whole passage where Paul is writing about men and women worshiping God together, under the lordship of Jesus and about God being glorified through that worship. Once you get past the cultural stuff regarding head covering and length of hair, there is a deep truth to be found here.

The truth I'm talking about is found in the word *glory*. The Greek word for glory that Paul uses here is *doxa*, which means "praise or ornamentation." So, Paul is making a case that men who are in Jesus, living their lives for Him, are literally God's ornaments of praise in this world. He made them personally from the dust, gave them life, and filled them with His image. Men are on the planet to make Him look good and to give Him glory. They are supposed to express His heart, His intentions, and His character. They should bring praise to Him by making a statement about who He is and what He is like.

Women, on the other hand, are different. God made them by taking the first daughter, who was Eve, from out of Adam. Therefore, she was a creation of God, made through, or from man. She was a reflection of God, through her man. She was made of his DNA. His very life was in her. She was inextricably tied to and woven into him by the Creator. Wow! Do you see where I am going with this? The snake sure did. That's why he attacked and slithered into that first marriage, and he has been doing so ever since. He realized that if men and women, in the context of marriage, were in unity, then God was glorified and the couple would be satisfied. They were made to be in harmony with each other for Him, to express Him. They were His ornaments. When a man and woman are in unity with each other, God's glory fills the planet.

So do you want to bring glory to God? Then you need to cover, bless, be in unity with, and protect your wife…His daughter. Do you want glory, peace, and power in your home and in your life? Then make your wife feel safe. Protect her. Keep the slithering snake away from her. Fight that hissing demon on her behalf, and the two of you will be ornaments of His glory, bringing praise to Him.

I would venture to say that if you observed my wife, Lori, you'd see that she is an amazing ornament for God. She's confident, poised, and carries herself with a quiet strength. She's so amazing; I get better looking just standing next to her! Most people who meet her wonder how I got so lucky to have her as my wife. I wonder too. She is amazingly beautiful. Together we bring some serious praise to our King. I am so thankful that He gave me the gift of His daughter Lori.

I also need to tell you that I've not always been able to say what I just said. Remember, I was a knucklehead. I objectified Lori and the other women in my life. It wasn't until I had a daughter of my own that my eyes were opened. That experience not only opened my eyes, it changed them. Today I see Lori and all the rest of His daughters much differently than ever before.

I want to share with you four eye-opening discoveries I have made through the years that have helped me see His daughters differently, especially the one I married…

Eye-Opening Discovery #1: Things are better when we have Cavetime together.

This is imperative! I am embarrassed to tell you that I didn't have a consistent Cavetime with my wife until the last few years. This is inexcusable; it's out of order and not consistent with His design for Christian couples. What a knucklehead I was! There's no way on the planet that you can affirm, cover, and help your wife blossom into the daughter He wants her to be without coming together for a regular time with Him. If you'll apply the five stones of Cavetime from chapter 9, then you'll grow, hear His voice, and make a strong wall of a home for His glory...*together*.

I challenge you to...

1. **Practice Stone #1 and set a time when the two of you will *show up* together.** You (the man, the physical barrier, the border patrol agent) must initiate this. Pull out your calendar right now and set the date and time. Remember, what gets scheduled gets done. Show up, and show up again. This is where the whole process begins. And don't tell me you don't have the time. You went golfing last week. You hunted and fished; you watched a game. You'll always make what is important to you a priority in your life. Is showing up together important enough for you to make it one of your top priorities? It should be. It has to be. If you want to be an ornament of praise for Him, it must be.

2. **Practice Stone #2 and *worship together.*** Get a favorite worship CD or playlist, read a Psalm (I suggest Psalms 23, 27, 34, or 144), or do something else together where you raise your voices in praise to God with His daughter, your wife. Take the first 5–10 minutes of your Cavetime together to make worship a focus. When you do that, the other stones will fall naturally into place.

3. **Practice Stone #3 and *pray together.*** For this stone I'm going to suggest you buy a journal and keep a list of things you two are going to pray for. Write down categories (i.e., children's names, family members' names, church issues, etc.), then list specific requests that

fall within those categories. It doesn't need to be a long and drawn out process, just a few key words that will help you remember what to pray for. I suggest you (the man) take the lead in writing these things down because it shows your wife that you care and that you're engaged. If you'd like to study types and methods of prayer to take your understanding and application of this stone a little deeper, here are a few suggestions:

- *Moving Mountains*, by John Eldredge. This is simply the best book that I have ever read on the subject of prayer.
- *Cavetime*, by Jeff Voth, especially the "Tool Belt" section.
- *The Sling*, by Jeff Voth. This book is a practical manual for implementation of all five stones, especially prayer.

4. **Practice Stone #4, and read the Word together.** For this stone I suggest you agree on a Bible verse or verses you want to read together (for example, maybe a verse from Sunday's sermon or a verse from one of the apps you've downloaded or a favorite verse of yours or your wife's). Read the verse or verses aloud. After you have read them, answer the following questions:

- What is the main truth contained in this passage?
- How does this main truth bring us closer together as a married couple?
- How can we apply the main truth practically in our marriage?

Remember, the focus of this eye-opening discovery is your relationship with His daughter, your wife, so I want you to look at the verses you chose through that lens. This is how you apply the force and power of the Bible to a specific area of your life.

I also want to encourage you to use your prayer journal to write down your answers and then pray about them aloud. Ask Jesus to bring alive the truths you each identified from the Word. This causes you to begin to internalize the truth of the Word together. You're becoming a strong wall, and because you're doing this together, it's also a beautiful wall. Your marriage is coming alive, going deep and growing strong and beautiful. The two of you are a beautiful wall for Him.

Eye-Opening Discovery #2: We should read a marriage book together.

This is a discovery I wish I'd made earlier because it's helped Lori and me immensely. It has unified us and brought us together in a powerful way. Reading together helps the two of you connect intellectually, spiritually, and relationally. If you want to grow strong in your marriage, you will need to connect on these levels with your wife. You read books on how to improve your backswing in golf, how to call ducks, invest in the market, or where to take a vacation. Why wouldn't you read a book on the second most important relationship in your life?

I know what you're thinking. You think a book that focuses on your marriage will be boring. Let me be blunt and speak to you in terms I promise you'll understand. If you want other things in your relationship to be strong, powerful, and hot (yes, I'm referring to what you think I am), then you should read with her! Read a lot with her.

At first, reading sounds kind of tough, because we all read at different speeds. Some of us can't stay locked in too long on a book or we get sleepy. So Lori and I have worked out a system that's been very helpful to us. We read a book together, but we don't read it at the same time. Let me explain.

After years of pleading with me to read a marriage book with her, I purchased one that came highly recommended by a marriage counselor friend of mine entitled, *Love and War* by John and Stasi Eldredge. I read the first chapter and highlighted a few things. I used the margins to write notes to myself as well as notes to Lori. Then I took our prayer journal (the one we use for Cavetime) and wrote a couple of thoughts that the first chapter provoked in me. I finished with a short, written prayer for our marriage. Then I took the book and the journal and laid it on the chair in her office where she has Cavetime each morning. I asked her to read the chapter from the book along with my notes. I suggested that she make her own notes, respond to my thoughts in the journal, and then return both the book and journal to me. Then I moved on to the next chapter and repeated the process until we finished the book.

This discovery has been eye opening, mind opening, and relationally amazing in the way it's affected us as a couple. This process of reading together has spurred conversation, prayer, and laughter. I'll bet we've said at least a hundred times, "Can you believe that the Eldredges have gone through that? That's just like us!" Through this process our relationship has been strengthened just knowing that we're not alone in our journey. In fact, we now call the Eldredges "the best friends we've never really hung out with."

I recommend this process to you and your wife, and John and Stasi's book is a great book to start with. I pray that Jesus will be with you as you read a book together. May your love for each other grow hot.

Eye-Opening Discovery #3: I should date my wife again.

> *O my dove, in the clefts of the rock, in the crannies of the cliff, let me see your face, let me hear your voice, for your voice is sweet, and your face is lovely.*
> —Song of Solomon 2:14, ESV

This is yet another discovery I wish I would've made earlier in my marriage. It would've saved thousands of dollars in counseling fees, stress, arguing, and wondering if we were going to make it as a couple. Did you read the above verse? Solomon wrote it, yeah, Solomon, the wisest man who ever lived. He was a serious player, wasn't he? You should read some of the other stuff he wrote in the Song of Solomon. Wow!

Let me guess…you used to write stuff like that to your wife too, didn't you? You just don't want to admit it now. She used to inspire the poet in you, right? You used to dream about her too. And then, after weeks, months, or years, she said yes, and you married her. Mission accomplished…at least in your mind.

That "mission accomplished" attitude, at least when it comes to romance between a husband and a wife, is actually a fire extinguisher. If you've fooled yourself into thinking that now that you're married, all you have to do to prove your love is pay for a roof over her head and groceries in the pantry, you're an idiot. Yes, I said it. But there's more.

You're a *knuckleheaded* idiot. A roof overhead and groceries in the pantry are the things any responsible husband should provide. If you really do love her, you'll be willing to do much more. There's no glory or ornamentation that comes from just providing the least amount possible. If the fire isn't out already, it's really close. You're aiming a fire extinguisher directly at it right now.

If you want to change the way you think about your marriage and if you want her to be fired up about being your wife, you need to invest in the things that won her heart over to begin with. You need to start dating again. Hey, it should be easy. The two of you were fired up about each other at one time, right? So it stands to reason that if the spark isn't sparking much anymore, start sparking again! Ask her out on a real date, and start the courtship all over again.

When did you start thinking that the mission was accomplished? Why did you stop dating? Was it the cares and toils of life? Was it a difficult situation you were faced with as a couple?

Was it the kids?

Was it some combination of the above?

Was it something else altogether?

Lori and I have made a commitment to pursue each other. Pursuing is more than just living together or tolerating each other. Pursuing is much more than just being roommates or business partners. One day we looked at each other and said, "There's got to be more than just this, living together, going to separate jobs, and taking care of the kids. We used to be fired up about each other, and now there isn't much of a flicker left. We've got to invest in our marriage, or we may not make it. What should we do?"

The answer to this question may be different for every couple, but the principle is the same. If you don't pursue each other and fan the flame of passion for each other, the flame will flicker out. This puts cracks and holes in the wall of your marriage and home together. You know what happens next, the snake slithers in unchallenged. And that's why so many couples are no more than business partners who stay together because their business is raising their kids. Then, when the kids are gone and the business has been accomplished, there's no longer a reason to stay together. You can stick a fork in them, they're done. I have seen this scenario repeated too many times, and I'm sure you have too.

Here is a simple three-step plan to ignite that spark and start dating again:

- **Step #1:** The first step is easy, take the initiative and ask your wife out on a date. I recommend taking your wife out at least once or twice per month. It doesn't have to be fancy or expensive. In fact, simple is often better. Just the fact that you've taken a bold step toward her will begin the sparking process. But don't get discouraged if the sparks don't fly right away. It took a while for the spark to be extinguished; it might take a while to get it going again. Keep at it. Don't quit, just keep showing up. Here are three great resources to help you with some creative dating ideas:

  - *20 Ideas for Dating Your Wife* by Justin Buzzard (http://www.familylife.com/articles/topics/marriage/staying-married/husbands/20-ideas-for-dating-your-wife)

  - *Spark Up Your Marriage* by The Art of Manliness (http://www.artofmanliness.com/2008/01/04/spark-up-your-marriage-6-ways-to-date-your-wife-all-over-again/)

  - *Dating Your Spouse* by Focus on the Family (http://www.focuson-thefamily.com/marriage/dating-your-spouse)

- **Step #2:** Leave her a handwritten note, send a text, or make a call to tell her that you love her. Do this at least once a day. Do whatever it takes to remember this, and make it a habit. Put an alarm on your phone; leave a note in your car, etc. Don't be tempted to stop just because she doesn't leave you notes as well. That's a weak excuse, guys. You're the man, and you have the stones. You're a wall. Walls stand, and then stand some more. Keep standing and sparking, and eventually a fire will be kindled.

- **Step #3:** Remember that small gifts pay big relational dividends. This may seem small, but it's huge! You know your wife better than anyone. What does she like? What does she think about? What will make her feel amazingly appreciated? A while back, my wife got a new flavor of ice cream after dinner at our favorite local restaurant. She almost fainted as she *ooh'd* and *aah'd* about how good it was. It was almost embarrassing. You can bet I made a note to myself, "Go out and get her some of that ice cream as a gift this week." She was very appreciative. My gift to her let her know that I was listening. Of course, it was kind of hard not to with the fuss she made! Sometimes it's the subtle, minor things that you do that say to her, "I was watching you and listening. I hear the little things you say." These little, quiet things you do for her scream *I love you!* So study her, my brother. And before you know it, the Holy Spirit Himself will be helping you, and a red-hot fire will be kindled.

Eye-Opening Discovery #4: Nakedness is good.

Then the man said,
"This at last is bone of my bones and flesh of my flesh; she shall be called Woman, because she was taken out of Man."
Therefore, a man shall leave his father and his mother and hold fast to his wife, and they shall become one flesh. And the man and his wife were both naked and were not ashamed.
—GENESIS 2:23–25, ESV, EMPHASIS ADDED

The fourth and final eye-opening discovery I have made is…drumroll please…nakedness is good! No, this is not a cheap trick just to get your attention and make sure you're not asleep. We're really going to discuss nakedness, right here, right now. But it's not what you think. Stay with me here.

There's currently a reality show on television called "Naked and Afraid." It's a show that follows the journey of couples who are dropped into the wilderness and have to survive together. Oh, and…you guessed it, they're both naked. Thankfully the screen is blurred. This seems wrong in so many ways. I tried to watch the show one time, and it was so ridiculous I could only stand it for about five minutes. There's just no way any normal, sane man or woman would ever volunteer for that duty. "They should be ashamed of themselves" is the only thought that ran through my head as I watched. I was in shock and disbelief.

But, like driving slowly past a car wreck, I must admit that it was a little difficult to turn away or change the channel. I mean, I have been in the wilderness many times before, but to think of being there naked makes me want to laugh, cry, become itchy all over, then sweat profusely…all at the same time. There are just so many things that could go wrong. Bad weather, bad bugs, bad bears, bad spiders, bad ticks, bad reptiles…you get my drift. But Adam and Eve, before the fall, had none of these. There were no bad things at all. They were not only not "Naked and Afraid," they were "Naked and Not Ashamed"! What a way to exist. No worries, no fear, no shame.

In my opinion, the fact that they weren't clothed isn't even the most important point. I'm convinced that the Holy Spirit had Moses write this in Genesis 2:25 because He wanted us to see several deep and meaningful pictures. Not only were they unclothed and not ashamed, they had nothing to hide. There was no need to hide. Nothing was hidden or covered up. Adam and Eve were free with each other, for each other, and next to each other. They could talk, walk, and be with God in the cool of the day…all day…together.

But, because of the fall of Adam (remember, I blame him for this, not Eve) in Genesis 3, bad, murderous things were unleashed, and shame, fear, and death were birthed into the world. Now and forever, nakedness would be associated with shame and hiding. Adam and Eve could no longer be transparent with each other or in front of God. Sadness, shame, and hiding replaced transparency and openness.

You know what I'm *not* going to do? I'm not even going to talk of the pain, death, and curse found in Genesis 3. We all know it; we feel it and fight it every day. I'm not going to focus on how the first Adam lost it all by sitting there and watching his wife, God's daughter, be deceived by the snake. What I will do is remind you of how the Second Adam restores us to that transparent, naked and unashamed place with God and His girl, a place where they walked together in unashamed fashion with no bad stuff to intimidate, bring fear, or cause them to want to hide from Him or blame and fight with each other. Let me remind you of what Romans 5 says.

Therefore, as one trespass led to condemnation for all men, so one act of righteousness leads to justification and life for all men. For as by the one man's disobedience the many were made sinners, so by the one man's obedience the many will be made righteous…as sin reigned in death, grace also might reign through righteousness leading to eternal life through Jesus Christ our Lord.

—Romans 5:18–19, 21, esv

So how does all this "naked talk" relate to Lori and me, and to you and your wife? Here's how. Because of the grace expressed to us in Jesus, who is the Second Adam, the transparency and shameless existence that was Adam and Eve's in the Garden, is available to you and your wife, only better. You can be transparent, open, real, and unashamed when you both are walking with Jesus and making room for Him to walk with you. What I'm telling you is that there is the possibility for a transparent, spiritual, and relational nakedness that's heavenly. You can find that place where you can walk with your wife and not be ashamed, a place of grace and restoration that's beautiful, precious, and untainted. It's just like what the first Adam and Eve experienced in the Garden, only more beautiful because Jesus is there and He will never, ever fail or fall. He is victorious over the snake every time.

Here are a few steps you can take to be free, transparent, and unashamed with your wife…

1. Ask the Second Adam (Jesus) to help you be transparent, honest, open, and free with your wife.

2. Ask Jesus to show you any areas in your life/marriage where you haven't been open and transparent with your wife. Tell Him how sorry you are. Ask Him how to share these things with her. Then be obedient to what He tells you to do.

3. Ask your wife if she needs to be transparent with you about anything, then let her share with you. Forgive her if necessary.

4. Take your wife's hands in yours, then together ask Jesus to deal with and heal both of you in the areas where you haven't been transparent

with one another. Tell each other that you forgive each other and are committed to walk in transparency and freedom. Kiss each other. Get ready to feel a spark. If you do, it might be time for nakedness!

I fully expect that as you and your wife, His daughter, practice this type of unashamed transparency, that you will walk in strength, power, and freedom, and that it will be life-giving to you and your people. Together, you will be a beautiful wall.

Chapter 13

If You Have a Daughter

"The well-fathered daughter is also the most likely to have relationships with men that are emotionally intimate and fulfilling. During the college years, these daughters are more likely than poorly-fathered women to turn to their boyfriends for emotional comfort and support and they are less likely to be "talked into" having sex. As a consequence of having made wiser decisions in regard to sex and dating, these daughters generally have more satisfying, more long-lasting marriages. What is surprising is not that fathers have such an impact on their daughters' relationships with men, but that they generally have *more* impact than mothers do. Their better relationships with men may also be related to the fact that well-fathered daughters are less likely to become clinically depressed or to develop eating disorders. They are also less dissatisfied with their appearance and their body weight. As a consequence of having better emotional and mental health, these young women are more apt to have the kinds of skills and attitudes that lead to more fulfilling relationships with men."[1]

If you were to watch my daughter and me when we're together, you could easily see our special relationship. In chapter 1 I told you the reason for this...since the day she was born she's touched my heart in a way it's never been touched before. Immediately, there was a protective instinct aroused within me; a whole new set of emotions began to spring to life, emotions that had never been allowed to grow before. Before my Hannah came along, I was like so many other fathers, just a young knucklehead who needed to learn to treat women differently. In my case, God's strategy was to use this one little girl to help make sure it happened. Hannah Jeanne would help the Lord and Lori with my transformation into a wall. It would take a while. In fact, their work isn't complete to this day. I'm still learning. But the process is one I've enjoyed, and I'm thankful to the Lord for it.

If you met Hannah, you'd notice right away that she's about one hundred pounds of beautiful…a beautiful lioness that is. She has a way of dealing with her brothers and her husband that's strong and determined on the one hand while being innocent and cute on the other. Of course Hannah Jeanne has captured my heart. The rest of my family easily sees that she can say and do stuff to me that no one else on the planet could get away with, and I think it's cute. She's been bossing me around since she was old enough to boss, and that wasn't very old. I cherish the connection we share; it's truly a blessing from God.

I want to share with you the five most important daddy things I have learned as a result of my relationship with her.

Daddy Thing #1:
I Told Her She Was the Prettiest Girl in the World

Hannah Jeanne, beauty queen, pertiest girl I've ever seen. No one pertier than my Hannah Jeanne.

Wordsworth it ain't, but the words of that silly poem I made up spoke to my daughter, Hannah, in a profound way. For as long as I can remember, I would sing this to her, and she knew in her heart that I meant every word. When I sang it, with a Southern drawl (and being raised in Colorado, the accent was far from authentic), she would look at me, roll her eyes, flip her little pigtails or pony tail and say, "Oh, Dad!"

But I'm telling you; those words spoke to her heart, her psyche, and the deepest parts of her little, emerging womanhood. I'm convinced that a little girl gets a huge amount of her self-esteem, sexual health, and hope for a healthy marriage from her daddy, and as the quote at the beginning of this chapter shows, I've got evidence to prove it. Listen up when I say this: "Dad, if you're not doing your job, there's always someone willing to step in (or should I say slither in) and inform those parts of her body and her soul."

I was convinced of the power of this message one particular day when Lori received a phone call from the mother of two of Hannah's little girl-friends. Hannah was only about five or six at the time and had been playing at her friend's house. Evidently, Hannah had deeply offended her two friends by telling them that she was the "prettiest girl in the world" and that they were not. Hannah explained to her friends that while they were cute, they were not "the prettiest."

Understandably the girls took issue with this, they began to cry and insist that she was wrong. Hannah, never one to back away, continued to try to convince them that it was true. In fact, she told them, her daddy even had a song that said she was the prettiest girl in the world. She asked her friends if their daddy had a song like her daddy did. When they told her no, I'm sure Hannah flipped her little ponytail at them and skipped away, case closed.

Lori and the girls' mother eventually got things squared away, and I don't think the little girls were scarred too much by the interaction with their confident, "prettiest" friend. I love that story. It's funny, but it reveals something about Hannah's frame of mind, don't you think? Do you see the power of a father's words as you hear that story? Even though Hannah would always roll her beautiful little eyes at me when I sang to her, she was catching every single word. Our daughters are listening, no matter how young they might be. All His daughters are listening.

Make it a point to tell all your girls that they are the "prettiest" and make sure you treat them that way. Remember, they are all His daughters. God has designed a powerful weapon to counteract the perverted culture we live in, a culture that seeks to only objectify, use, and abuse our daughters. What's that weapon? Your voice! So speak to their hearts, sing to them; let them know they're the prettiest to you, no matter what anyone else says. If you'll do this, they won't even hear the hisses of snakes.

Daddy Thing #2:
I Respected Her Mom in Front of Her

I'm the first to say that my journey to becoming a wall has been a long and drawn out process. I'm also quick to say, I've still got a long way to go. But I've always done my best to honor and respect Lori in front of Hannah. By this I mean that I have regularly tried to compliment and affirm Lori in ways that Hannah can see and hear. This hasn't been hard. Lori has always deserved my compliments and fully expected me to respond to her in a positive way. I wanted that for Hannah too; I wanted her to expect the compliments from me just as Lori did. I always wanted Hannah to think that this is how it's supposed to be between a woman and the husband she loves. I wanted her to have the picture in her mind that her husband would compliment and affirm her just the way I did with her mother. After all, she is the "pertiest girl in the world."

Daddy Thing #3:
Hate All Boys

I know the heading to this section sounds a bit harsh, but let me explain. While I don't really hate all boys, I'm keenly aware of what many men, especially men in our culture, would like to do to my daughter. I'm a man myself, and I know the way men think; I know what's in their hearts. And believe me, without the redemptive help of Jesus, I would be thinking the very same way about His daughters. The Bible says this about Jesus's knowledge of men's hearts:

> *But Jesus on his part did not entrust himself to them, because he knew all people and needed no one to bear witness about man, for he himself knew what was in man.*
> —JOHN 2:24–25, ESV, EMPHASIS ADDED

Hey, I'm being straight up honest here. There are many guys who would like to do bad things to our girls—to my girl. And I just took the simplified position that I didn't like any of them. And I wouldn't like any of them until they could prove to me that they were worthy of even being in the same room with her. I was the border patrol agent, the watchdog, the one who would strike you down if you touched my little girl inappropriately. I would bare my teeth and growl at you if you got too close or looked at her with impure motives in your eyes. One time I caught a guy looking Hannah up and down while we were in a convenience store, and you can bet I had a stare down with that guy. If you've ever heard the phrase, "If looks could kill…" then you've probably got a pretty good idea of the way I was looking and even growling at him. You may be laughing to yourself thinking I'm joking, but I'm deadly serious. Do not mess around with one of my girls.

We need some men who will stand as a wall for their little girls, little girls who will one day grow up into beautiful girls. From the time Hannah was little, she knew I was her "boyfriend." I was the one male who would spend time with her and cherish her. But she always knew that one day I would give her, my precious gift (I've always called her my Rose) to a man who was "better than me." When I say, "better than me," that's exactly what I mean. I want my daughter to find a man who is better than me, more selfless than me, more Christlike, more godly, even more committed to standing as a wall for all women than I have been. I want Hannah to find a man who is more relentless in his love for her than I have been. Hard to find? You bet. I know that's going to be a tall order to fill, and that's as it should be. These goals are very important to me. They mean life and death to me.

But until we met the one, I chose to hate all the others, growling at them when they wandered too close. I was protecting my Rose so she would be saved for the one. I always knew, without question, that if I was ever called on, I would risk my life for her. I would tell my little girl Hannah these things as she grew up; she knew I meant what I said. Of course she probably thought I was crazy, but she knew I had a deep love for her, put there by God. She also knew that she had a Heavenly Father, and she knew she was His daughter.

I know that this language may sound a little harsh and extreme, but I use these words on purpose. It was necessary for Hannah and me, and it worked. She is an amazing young woman, and she knows her daddy loves her. I'm convinced that our girls today need fathers who will stand for them until the better man comes into their lives. Throughout this book I have provided you with plenty of statistics and stories to support the fact that the snake is slithering, doing whatever he can to steal your daughters. Do you still think my ways and my words are extreme? I don't think so!

Daddy Thing #4:
Conduct the Interview

I have heard men joke around about making sure they're cleaning their guns when a guy shows up at their house to pick up their daughter for a date. Other guys talk about making the young suitor submit to a rigorous interview. While I'm sure there are those who have done these things, I've yet to actually meet one. I haven't done the "gun cleaning" thing (although it sounds fun!), but I have conducted a couple of interviews as Hannah and I engaged in the dating scene. By interviews, I mean being intentional about having a conversation, preferably face-to-face, with any guy who wishes to spend time building a relationship with my daughter.

Once again, you might laugh about the "engaging in the dating scene" statement, but I'm serious. This is one of the most important processes your daughter will ever participate in. How could you not be involved? Why would you not be involved? Brother, I'm telling you, man-to-man, dad-to-dad, you've got to step up here. You need to be the one to help her choose the one God has marked for her. He will be the one who will love her as much as you do, maybe even more, which I know sounds impossible to you now. Remember, there are probably lots of guys out there who might try to pursue your daughter, but they are incapable of loving her as much as you do. And that's not the kind of guy you want for her.

And God doesn't want that for her either. There are also those guys who would love the chance to use and objectify her. These are exactly the kinds of guys that God wants you to protect her from. Your little girl needs you to walk with her through these processes, all of them, dating, engagement, and marriage. These processes are powerful parts of your journey together, ones that will have a direct impact on the legacy God wants to leave through you and your daughter.

Since I can't give you any pointers on the gun strategy for weeding out the bad guys who might want to date your daughter, I'll have to stick to advice about the interview. Here are my five important interview steps:

1. Start dating your daughter while she is still your little girl.

By this I mean you should take her out and have special time with just her. Open doors for her, buy special little gifts just for her, treat her like your princess. This will set the stage for what she can expect from men as she grows older. Whenever she's not treated the way you treated her, it will be a clear red flag for her.

2. Never forget how powerful your words are. Shower her with words of positive affirmation every time you're with her. I have included some suggestions here for you.

a. Remind her that you are her first "boyfriend."

b. Tell her how much you cherish her…how much you want to spend time with her.

c. Tell her that one day you will give her, your precious gift, to a man who will be "better than you," and there is only one of those out there. Tell her that until the time he comes into the picture you will be suspicious of all others.

d. I call my daughter, Hannah, my "Rose." Do you have a special name for your daughter? Special names make your daughter feel special.

e. Tell her that you are protecting her, your _____ (special name), so that she will be saved for the man who will be better than you.

f. Tell her that you would risk your life for her if you had to.

g. Tell her that you have a crazy deep love for her, put there by God, her Heavenly Father, and that she is ultimately His daughter.

You need to understand that years and years of showering your daughter with positive affirmation will set the stage for what's coming in Step 3. Your daughter must know that you care and that she is more precious to you than your own life. If she doesn't know this in her core, Step 3 will seem like a major intrusion to her.

3. When your daughter is of dating age (which I would define as 14–18 years old) let her know that any young man who wants to ask her on a date needs to come and personally ask you first.

This means that the young man needs to call and ask to speak with you in person. No hiding behind a text or email here. If a face-to-face, eyeball-to-eyeball meeting can't be set up, a phone call is the next best thing.

As you engage with your daughter and potential suitors in this manner, everyone involved in her dating process will know that anyone who wants to spend time with your daughter is answerable directly to you. In our case, Hannah was appreciative (eventually), because she knew I cared about her. She admitted to me that it seemed overbearing at first, but eventually our process made her feel safe.

One time I heard there were some guys giving her trouble at school about our dating process. Immediately my protective instinct kicked in. I was ready for battle, but I took a few deep breaths. When I calmed down a little, I came up with a better idea. I volunteered (Hannah says I threatened) to come spend the day with her. I could walk her to class and take a seat in the hallway outside each classroom for the day. I was willing to do this every day…until the problem went away. She knew I wasn't kidding around. Her friends knew too. The word was out…Hannah was not to be messed with. In the end, I only had to threaten a couple of the teenage boys before the problem went away.

Our mandatory interview process helped Hannah eliminate the riff-raff she wouldn't have spent time with anyway. All she had to do was tell them that they had to call her dad and 99 percent of them didn't have the stones to make the call. I have heard several stories about guys who found out about the call and the interview and were not about to pursue her.

That's exactly what I was shooting for. I wanted those guys to be afraid. I wanted a process in place that would intimidate them. I wanted them to see the look on my face whenever they thought about my daughter. I wasn't fooling around. I was the border patrol agent, guarding Hannah for the man who was going to come along who would be better than me.

4. When a young man calls or meets with you personally, here are some suggested questions to be asked. Suggested interview questions:

Why do you want to spend time with my daughter?

This is important. He should be able to articulate to you why he wants to spend time with your girl. Is it just to "chill on the couch"? Play video games? Go clubbing? I don't think so. Interview over. Before anyone is going to spend time with my daughter, he's going to have to have more of a plan than that.

What are you like?

Any prospective date should be able to describe himself. Is it all about physicality? Is it all about money? Who is he? Is he all about himself, "smoking his own dope"? Or is he about others?

What are you doing with your life?

Does the young man have a plan for his future? Does he want to further his education? Is he employed? What kind of work does he do? How does his current job fit in with his future career plans? The answers he gives to these questions will give you some valuable insight into his initiative and sense of purpose.

Tell me about your family?

Who are his parents? What do they do? Are they married? Divorced? Where are they from? Does he have siblings? His answers to these questions will help you get a bead on what his example of "normal family life" has been. What is his normal?

Do you drink alcohol?

This is a very important piece of information. If he drinks, can he tell you why? How often? Where? For me…if the guy drank alcohol, it was a deal-breaker. What if he encouraged your daughter to drink or thought it was okay to get into a car with a driver who had been drinking…and putting your daughter at that kind of risk! Too many young people die because of this one. If you let your girl date a guy who answers yes to this question, there are a few things I would like to say to you, but they'd never get past the editor. Just suffice it to say that I think you're an idiot.

Do you smoke?

If he says yes, then the follow-up question has to be, "What do you smoke and why?" You need to know that if he smokes cigarettes and/or cigars that they can be gateway habits for marijuana, which can lead to all kinds of other bad stuff. Needless to say, a yes to this question would be a deal-breaker for me too.

Where are you planning to take my daughter? Why?

This question is also a very important one. Does he want to take her to a movie? To have dinner? To a party? Where will they be and how long will they be there? The guy needs to know that if he tells you one thing but does something else that you might just consider your girl kidnapped. And in that case, all bets are off as to what you might do. Once again, I am not joking around here. Sadly, we live in a time when we must know who our daughters are with, where they're going, and what they're doing.

When do you plan on having my daughter home?

This should go without saying, but I'm going to mention it here. Ideally, the young man should bring this up before you have to, but just in case he doesn't, you should have a reasonable curfew in mind that you've already agreed to with your daughter. Once the time has been set, it's up to the young man to respect the decision of you and your daughter.

Do you know Jesus personally?

Once again, this question should go without saying. Any man who spends time with your daughter should know and love Jesus Christ. I encourage you to be bold enough to ask him point blank. If he doesn't know Jesus, it might just be a great time to ask him if he wants to. You and your daughter will need to decide if this is a deal-breaker or not.

If the young man answers these questions to your satisfaction, then the next step is to make sure he knows that the final decision is up to your daughter. This gives you a chance to let her know how the interview went and to pray with her about whether or not she should spend time with him.

Brother, in today's over-sensualized and over-sexualized culture, a protective barrier has to be created between other men and your daughter. I can't emphasize that enough. Your precious little girl needs to be guarded, protected, and made secure for the man you will eventually give her away to on the day of her wedding. She is the most precious gift you have on this planet, your daughter, His daughter.

Daddy Thing #5:
Give Her to a Man Who Is Better Than You

The final of my *five most important daddy things* is really just the reward for stepping up and engaging in the first four things. By that I mean, if we pursue these things faithfully, we will be protecting, guarding, and preparing our daughters for the man they will hopefully walk with for many years. Your little girl, His daughter, will grow into a powerful lioness…a warrior princess, ready to live with and love a man who is *better than you.*

Mark

I remember when Mark first appeared on my radar. I was convinced he was one of many young college men drawn to my powerful preaching. Our young church was exploding with young men just like Mark, and I was honored to be their mentor and leader. I knew he was hanging around the church just hoping to spend more time with me. Like a knucklehead, I thought I was the attraction, that I was The Man.

And here was Mark, a manly young man responding to a manly man in an effort to be mentored in godly manliness. I understood. He was a little shy. He never approached me directly, nor did he speak to me when he had the chance. He did, however, seem to be hanging around on the fringes of the crowd looking in. I assumed he was just introverted and intimidated by my powerful manly presence.

Then one Sunday, in a quick glance, I thought I saw Mark pass Hannah in the hallway and notice her before heading out into the crowded parking lot. At the time I thought nothing of it. But later that week I overheard a discussion between Hannah and her brothers. As I leaned in to listen I realized that they were chiding her about some boy she was interested in. As I listened more closely, I heard one of her brothers say, "He doesn't even know you exist, Hannah. He's in college, and you're only fifteen."

The Prettiest One flipped her ponytail and said, "Oh, he sees me all right. And I'm going to grow up and marry him someday."

The boys shouted in unison, "No way! He's way too old for you! He's a *man!*"

"Marry who?" I asked.

Hannah gave her ponytail another flip and shot back, "Mark Pepin."

On that day I didn't really give the exchange much thought. Hannah was just a fifteen-year-old girl daydreaming about a crush. I figured the boys were probably right; Hannah probably wasn't even on Mark's radar. After all, he was there to hear me preach and be mentored from a distance. I shrugged it off and forgot about it.

Well, to make a long story short, today, the Prettiest, my Hannah is in fact, Mrs. Mark Pepin. To my chagrin, it soon became apparent that he was not there because of my preaching. He can't even remember one sermon that I preached from those years. He wasn't following me around hoping I'd say something profound. He wasn't looking for a mentor.

The fact was, he had noticed my beautiful young daughter who was on the worship team and kept hanging around the church hoping she'd notice him. But he knew the rules, he knew how involved I was in Hannah's dating process and knew she wouldn't be allowed on a car date until she turned eighteen, especially with an "old man" like Mark. But he was a good man, a patient man who was willing to wait. Or in his own words, "I didn't want to be seen as an old creeper. So I waited."

Mark waited a lot longer than three weeks or three months. He waited three long years just hoping and praying that Hannah wouldn't fall for anyone else. He knew that with Hannah, there was the potential for marriage.

What a good man! Mark is a better man than me. There's no way I would wait for three years. Heck, I had a hard enough time waiting three months! But again, I was a knucklehead. Good men know how to be patient for the things God has for them. Good men know how to wait.

The Call

One day I received a phone call from a number I didn't recognize. I let it go to voicemail. Later, when I got the chance to listen to the message, it was none other than Mark Pepin. For those of you who don't know Mark, today he is a fiery, animated preacher and leader. But back then he wasn't fiery at all; in fact, he was a bit of a wallflower. Sometimes he fumbled and stumbled, and his voice would crack. His message was brief and to the point. He said his name and asked if I would call him back…his voice cracking the whole way. I sensed fresh meat and planned for my surprise attack carefully. I would call him back and act as if I didn't know who he was. That would set him back on his heels a bit. I figured I'd roll that out and then see where the conversation went.

Mark answered the phone, "Hello?"

"Yeah, this is Jeff Voth. I got a call from this number. Who is this?"

"Uh…um, It's Mark…."

"Who? I'm sorry. I don't know a Mark. Mark who?"

Now, of course, I knew exactly who it was. Mark's name was a familiar one in our house; Hannah and her brothers had been arguing about him for almost three years. Gradually there was talk that he was as interested in Hannah as she was in him, but he hadn't really played his hand yet. The name was also familiar because I knew a couple of his brothers. Mark was the youngest of ten kids, and a pastor doesn't overlook a family in his church with ten kids.

Over the phone I could hear him nervously clearing his throat and trying to get his breathing under control.

I found out later that Mark, who is a very logical guy and a real planner, had actually prepared notes and had his whole speech written out. But I'd tripped him up; he had nothing in his notes to prepare him for me not knowing who he was.

It wasn't time yet to let him off the hook, "Now who is this again?"

"It's Mark Pepin. I'm Brad's brother."

"I'm sorry, I'm still not getting a picture of who you are. I mean the Pepins take up a whole section of the church. There must be a hundred people in that family. Hey, describe yourself to me. What do you look like?"

"Huh? Um, I have brown…."

I could tell I really had him going. The breathing was getting quicker, and I could tell his mouth was bone dry. I could hear his tongue sticking to the top of his mouth.

"Is your head big?"

"What?"

"Do you have a large head?"

"Um, I think it's regular sized."

"Compare your head size to something. Cantaloupe? Watermelon? Football?"

He didn't know what to do. I sensed that at any given time he might faint or vomit, so I eased up a bit and finally let him off the hook.

"Mark?"

"Yes."

"Mark, I know who you are."

"Really? Oh God…Pastor Voth…Why did you do that? I feel sick. God…."

Then there was silence. I think he may have forgotten why he called. Shock may have been setting in a bit. More silence.

"Mark, what's up? How can I help you?"

"Um, Pastor Voth, I know that Hannah turns eighteen in a week, and I wondered if it would be okay if I took her out on a date."

I didn't say yes right away. I just had to work him a little bit more.

"Hmm, do you think she wants to go out with you?"

"What? Well, I don't know. Do you know?"

"I'm not sure, Mark. You'll have to ask her yourself. But you have my permission to take her out on a date if she wants to go out with you."

"Thank you, sir. Wow, that was rough!"

I couldn't resist one last bit of pressure, "Mark?"

"Yes, sir."

"Mark, I'm a pretty old-fashioned guy. I feel that when a man comes to ask to spend time with another man's daughter, he should bring him a gift of some kind. It's an Old Testament thing. So if she says yes to a date, I'll expect a gift. Like a dowry, but not as big of a deal."

"What kind of a gift would you like, sir?"

I knew I was pushing him to the edge, I could hear exasperation in his voice. The poor guy just wanted to get off of the phone.

"Oreos."

"Oreos?"

"What kind of Oreos? Regular or Double Stuff?"

"Surprise me."

Mark not only stepped up and brought them on the first date, he continued to bring Oreos for so long I finally had to tell him to stop. I ate Oreos solid for a year and never had to pay for a single package. Hannah had obviously said yes.

After their courtship Mark called me again. We agreed to meet at Starbucks, across from Arvada High School in Arvada, Colorado. We sat down and looked at each other eyeball-to-eyeball. That's when he asked if I would give him Hannah's hand in marriage. It was an amazing, powerful, holy exchange; an exchange where I gave my daughter to a better man, the man we'd been waiting for since she was a little girl.

Chapter 14

If You're Single

I'm a happily married guy. So happily, in fact, that I can't even remember what it felt like to be single nor do I care! So, how can a happily married guy like me write honestly about what a single guy needs to do in order to be a wall? The fact is, I can't. That's why I've reached out to a couple of single guys I share life with. I respect these guys greatly. I can vouch for them; they're men who take their stand every day as walls for His daughters.

Just so you know the process, I sat down with each of these guys and had a very open and honest conversation. Then I took the highlights from our conversations and wove them together here to make it easier for you to follow. If you're a single guy, I know their comments will be helpful to you. Heck, I think their comments will be helpful to you whether you're single or not.

1. How would you describe who His daughters are to someone who is totally out of the loop?

That's easy…all women are His daughters. And the "H" is capitalized on purpose because no matter who their earthly father is, they are God's daughters first. Every woman on the planet has been created in His image, given as a gift. God, the Heavenly Father, is their Daddy.

2. Describe what it means to be "a wall for His daughters."

First, it means that women don't belong to me; they belong to God. Therefore, every woman needs to be treated accordingly, like a daughter of the King. Every woman deserves to be treated like royalty because she is His daughter and He is the King and Creator of all. That's why women should be held in high esteem, respected at all times and not viewed as something I can possess and use for my own pleasure. Also, when I see a woman, I need to understand that she is not only His daughter but, chances are, she'll be someone else's wife someday. So not only do I need to respect His daughters, but I also need to respect the man who will ultimately be her husband. That guy, whoever he may be, is my brother. In the same way, I expect any man who spends time with the woman who will eventually be my wife to treat her with the same dignity and respect. I would be a total hypocrite if I didn't feel that way.

Secondly, being a wall for His daughters means I need to seek to protect them, physically, emotionally, and relationally. How do I protect them? By making sure our relationship doesn't get too deep. This is tough because it's so counter-intuitive. Our natural tendency as guys is to rush in to protect. When a weaker person is under an attack of any kind, it's natural for us guys to want to run to the rescue. The problem with that instinct is that when we do this, we naturally get close to them. And when we get close, there is the potential for a physical switch to get turned on, and that's when things can get dangerous. Things switch from the relational to the physical in a heartbeat, and suddenly that which was sacred has turned sexual. I'm sure you can see the problem: there she is, wanting to be relational because you cared for her, you rushed in to help in her time of need, but meanwhile your lever has been switched, and you find yourself getting fired up to be sexual with her. That's why we need to protect His daughters. We need to be careful not to get too close. We need Jesus to help us to stand as a wall while making sure we're not sending the wrong signals. There is a fine balance here, and since Jesus understands both sides perfectly, He is the perfect One to help us navigate these tricky waters. These daughters of His are to be protected, not used. It's difficult sometimes to find this balance, but it really is possible.

Third, I don't have the right to "pursue" anyone I want to. This may sound redundant, but it has to be mentioned again. All women belong to Him, not to me. I need to protect them all and only pursue the one I know He has for me.

3. Have you ever been guilty of objectifying His daughters? If so, how?

Yes, I have…in a couple of ways. First, I've lusted for women, whether it was looking at porn or watching women walk down the street. I have even lusted for women I've seen at church. But I'm proud to say I don't do these things nearly as much as I used to. I'm getting better and stronger every day. I'm growing in my understanding of the fact that every woman is His daughter and probably even another man's wife. I have no right to look at them as merely objects for my pleasure. I know it's wrong, and I'm doing better with Jesus's help.

Secondly, I know I've objectified women by my selfish desire to have a girlfriend. It doesn't really even matter who the girl is, I just seem to feel better about myself if I have someone to call mine. If I'm in a relationship with someone, texting her, emailing her, or calling her on the phone, I'm happier than when I'm alone. I've recently been convicted in my heart that this way of thinking is wrong. It's just using someone else to make me feel good while never taking into account how she might feel about it. While it doesn't feel dirty like porn or visually undressing a girl as she walks down the street, I still know it's wrong. I know I'm objectifying women. I'm so thankful that Jesus is there to help me with this.

4. What are four steps you've taken in your life to keep from objectifying His daughters?

Step #1 is to ask Jesus for His help…often. When I look at a girl lustfully I ask Him to help me. When I'm tempted to look at porn I ask Him to help me. When I feel that I might be getting too close in a relationship, I seek His guidance. When I sense that she wants more from me than I'm able to give her, I ask for God's help. Help me, Jesus!

Step #2 is to stay consistent in the Word and in prayer. This may sound like a cliché but that doesn't mean it's not true…and powerful. Stay in the Word and in prayer! During those times when I'm faithful to stand on God's Word I'm stronger, and my potential to be a wall for His daughters emerges more quickly and more often. But I crumble and fall whenever I fail to stay in the Word or to be faithful in prayer.

Step #3 is to remember that every girl is His little girl. She might fulfill several roles in her lifetime—sister, mother, wife, and daughter—but no matter the role, she'll always be His little girl. I have a sister, and I would be deeply offended if I knew she was being objectified. How can I even think about doing to someone else's little girl what I would never want done to mine? I ask Jesus every day to help me in this area. When it comes to the way I relate to His daughters, I don't want to be a hypocrite in thought or deed.

Step #4 is to make sure that I "stay surfaced." Once again this may sound counter-intuitive, but I'm going to share what works best for me. Be especially careful not to get too close. By this I mean that I don't think you should allow a female to become your best friend, sharing your deepest and most heartfelt feelings with her. This causes the two of you to wander into territory that, in my opinion, is reserved for married couples only. This brings me to my next "stay surfaced" point, which is prayer. I know that this might sound really weird, but I don't think that you should pray a lot with a girl one-on-one. Prayer is an intimate act and opens the two of you up into deep, relational ways. Don't share intimate space with a woman until Jesus gives you permission. That space belongs to Him. He owns you just like He owns every woman you'll ever meet. He knows the woman He wants you to open up to. So stay surfaced until He gives you permission to get close. Be a wall. Be a man who stands in responsible, healthy, and brotherly fashion.

I want to challenge you to consider these four steps along with the other strategies we've already discussed. As a single man, if you can do these things, you'll be taking strong and powerful steps toward being a wall for His daughters. I am proud of you. Together, you and Jesus can do this!

Chapter 15

Dance the Haka

The haka is a type of ancient Māori war dance traditionally used on the battlefield, as well as when groups came together in peace. Haka is a fierce display of a tribe's pride, strength, and unity. Actions include violent foot-stamping, tongue protrusions, and rhythmic body slapping to accompany a loud chant. The words of a haka often poetically describe ancestors and events in the tribe's history."[1]

The first time I saw a haka I wasn't exactly sure what I was watching. There was rhythmic stomping, men shouting in a language I didn't know, their tongues sticking out, and even a little spit running down their chins. Talk about bizarre! This particular haka took place before a rugby match between the legendary New Zealand All Blacks and some poor opponents who were reduced to standing and watching the spectacle in stark terror, something powerful and mysterious. For all intents and purposes, the match was over right there. I knew those poor guys were going to get beat. I'll admit I was mesmerized. And while I wasn't exactly sure what was being shouted, I could feel the waves of passion coming through the screen...it was palpable. I knew in my gut I was witnessing something primal.

I have since learned that the origin of the haka goes back to the culture of the Maori people of New Zealand. They are an ancient Polynesian people who have inhabited parts of New Zealand and have been performing the haka since around 1300 A.D. The Maori used the haka to tell stories, intimidate enemies, express their love for one another, and welcome esteemed guests. The Maori have been intentional about passing down this important cultural tradition from one generation to the next.

You know where I'm going with this, right? *I think we should be a living haka dance for our people, especially for His daughters!* (I am actually shouting and doing a haka as I write this!)

I can hear you saying to yourself, "What? Me, be a dance for my people? There's no way. I have no sense of rhythm." Don't worry, I'm not actually suggesting that you should go out and learn the haka, although it sounds totally fun to me. What I am saying is that as men we should take a lesson from the Maori. I'm saying that it wouldn't hurt us to get a dose of passion for our faith in Jesus and for the roles He's given us as the protectors of His daughters and a wall for His people. It wouldn't hurt us to live like warriors and do a war dance from time to time, especially on behalf of His daughters. There are enemies at the door right now, trying to steal and objectify them. Are you ready to do a haka?

I can't think of a better way for you to understand what I'm trying to describe than for you to see the haka dance that put me over the edge and made me a total haka fan. Here's a link to a past Cavetime conference in 2016 where I describe a haka dance that occurred spontaneously at the wedding of two young New Zealanders: https://youtu.be/TVbaw-rRIPk.

Do you see what I mean? How's that for scary passion?

How's that for making women feel safe enough to express themselves as the warrior princesses they were intended to be? How's that for making those women feel so safe and cared for and loved that all they could do was cry good tears?

For those of you who haven't watched the video yet, let me describe the scene as best I can, although I'm sure I can't come close to doing the video justice. The video was shot at the wedding of two young New Zealanders. At a certain point in the ceremony the brother of the bride stands up and begins to do a haka, yelling out words in the Maori language. The groom spontaneously joins in along with the groomsmen and several other men in the audience. Even some of the bridesmaids join in, which is unusual. Soon the bride is overtaken with emotion. She bursts into tears and begins to do the haka herself.[2] Here is the interpretation of what was said during the haka:

Leader: Pay attention. Listen up, take your stance!

Everyone: Hi!

Leader: Arms outstretched, out and back!

Everyone: Kss! Kss!

Leader: What is right is always right!

Everyone: Indeed!

Leader: What is right is always right!

Everyone: Ah…yes! Be true to yourself, my son! My concerns have been raised about you, so pay attention! What is this problem you are carrying? How long have you been carrying it? Have you got that? Right, let's go on.

Leader: So son, although it may be difficult for you, and son, although it seems to be unyielding no matter how long you reflect on it, the answer to the problem is here inside you. Indeed! Indeed! Indeed! Yes, indeed![3]

The words and steps in this haka are actually ones that young boys learn as they grow up in school in New Zealand. Therefore, when they are called on in battle, sporting events, family ceremonies, funerals, and other such occasions, they are able to step up and raise their masculine voices in unison, striking fear into their enemies and opponents, and passion into the hearts of their comrades and the ones they're standing for.

While the words are obviously important and meaningful to those in attendance, the most powerful aspect of this video to me was how the women responded. It is not typical for Maori women to participate in the haka, yet in this video they did, and you can tell by watching that they joined in with their whole hearts.

I read an interview with the bride from the video. Her name is Aliyah Armstrong. She confirmed that fact that most of the time women don't participate in the haka. Yet, when her bridesmaid was overcome with emotion and started to chant, then dance, all she could do was follow her lead. Then she wept tears of heartfelt joy. The video ends with the men rubbing noses in the traditional greeting called a Honji. After the Honji, worshipful, peaceful singing is heard at the conclusion of the ceremony.[4]

What a powerful example of men willing to raise their voices in unison, calling out to other men. And then their passion and fervor causing the women around them to be drawn in and touched by the fire as well. Then, as if that weren't enough, a sense of peace, calm, and safety descends, reassuring everyone that all is well.

Whether you understood this intimate peek inside the Maori culture or not, you can't deny the effect of their masculine passion on those who were in attendance at the wedding that day. Since the video was posted, it's gotten over thirty million views. Thousands have responded to the postings of the video on our own Cavetime social media sites. Fire. Power. Passion. Safety. Who doesn't want these things? Who can deny that we desperately need all these things in our own culture? Especially on behalf of our daughters.

Dance with Me

Will you do the haka with me? I'm convinced that we need to do this for our people. Maybe you will never dance a haka like those warriors did that day at the wedding, but you can dance the dance of faith over your people. You can stand as a wall for Jesus and raise your life and your voice on His behalf. I'm convinced that when we dance the dance of faith over them, our people will feel safe. When you make the decision to be a man of God in your culture and stand as a wall for His daughters, others will stand and dance with you. Others will hear your cries and see you stand and proclaim the power of God and the authority of His men as a wall. Others will hear you; they will make their way to you and start to dance alongside you.

I have written the words to a chant that I think would go great with a haka. Maybe you should stand up right where you are, pound your chest, stomp your feet, and repeat after me. I can't think of a more fitting way for us to finish this book together than standing as a wall for His daughters as we do a haka together chanting the following verse.

Me: He is The Rock, Our Living Stone.

You: On His behalf, we stand for you.

Me: He is The Rock; we are His sons.

You: On His behalf, we stand for you.

Me: He is The Rock; you will be safe.

You: On His behalf, we stand for you.

Me: He is The Rock; we are His sons.

You: On His behalf, we stand for you.

Me: He is The Rock; you are His daughters.

You: On His behalf, we stand for you.

Me: He is The Rock; you are His Gemstones.

You: You are His Beauty; we stand for you.

Me: He is our Rock; together we stand.

You: A beautiful wall, woman and man.

Me and **You** together: Hooah!

Endnotes

Chapter 2

1. John Haltiwanger, "Heroic Homeless Man Gave His Life to Save a Woman Being Held Hostage," *Elite Daily,* September 9, 2015, http://elitedaily.com/news/homeless-man-gives-life-save-woman-hostage-video/1206030/.

Section 2

1. https://www.ahistoryofgreece.com/biography/lycurgus.htm. Viewed online April 2017.

Chapter 3

1. Brand, C., Draper, C., England, A., Bond, S., Clendenen, E. R., & Butler, T. C., (Eds.). (2003). Bulwark. In *Holman Illustrated Bible Dictionary* (p. 243). Nashville, TN: Holman Bible Publishers.

2. Ibid. (p. 1365).

3. Numa Denis Fustel De Coulanges, *The Ancient City: A Study on the Religion, Laws and Institutions of Greece and Rome.* The Johns Hopkins University Press, Baltimore and London. 1980, p. 130.

4. Katie Abbey-Lambertz, "Most Dangerous Neighborhoods: Detroit Home to 3 Most Violent Areas in America," *The Huffington Post,* May 22, 2013.

5. Luke Manley, MPH, "The Eroding (OK, Eroded) Masculinity of the American Male," *Talking About Men's Health,* April 8, 2013, http://www.talkingaboutmenshealth.com/the-eroding-ok-eroded-masculinity-of-the-american-male/.

6. David Blankenhorn (1995). *Fatherless America: Confronting our Most Urgent Social Problem.* New York, NY: Basic Books.

7. Ray Williams, "The decline of fatherhood and the male identity crisis," *Psychology Today*, June 19, 2011, https://www.psychologytoday.com/ blog/wired-success/201106/the-decline-fatherhood-and-the-male-identity-crisis.

8. Lorena Mongelli, Kevin Sheehan, and Lia Eustachewich, "Elevator Hero Wished Woman 'Happy New Year' Before Being Crushed to Death," *New York Post*, January 1, 2016, http://nypost.com/2016/01/01/ young-man-crushed-to-death-by-elevator-cops/.

9. David D. Gilmore, *Manhood in the Making,* (Yale University Press, 1990), p. 226.

10. Ken Blackwell, "Boys Without Dads: A Cruel and Volatile Calculus," *Townhall*, May 11, 2015, http://townhall.com/columnists/ kenblackwell/2015/05/11/boys-without-dads-a-cruel-and-volatile-calculus-n1997090/page/full.

Chapter 5

1. David Gungor & John Arndt, The Brilliance, *Cavetime: A Worship Experience,* 2011.

2. Deborah Amos, "Online with a Sexual Predator," *ABCNews.com*, August 14, 2016, http://abcnews.go.com/WNT/story?id=130735&page=1.

Chapter 6

1. Richard and Linda Sauer, "Pornography: A Distortion of God's Plan," *Answers in Genesis,* March 29, 2007, https://answersingenesis.org/ morality/pornography-a-distortion-of-gods-plan/.

2. Statistics quoted from the Pure Hope website and found here: http:// www.purehopefoundation.com/awareness/.

3. Mariah Towner, "Man Saves Woman Trapped Inside SUV," DailyMail.com, June 16, 2015, http://www.dailymail.co.uk/news/article-3642544/Police-Man- saves-woman-trapped-inside-SUV-river.html.

Endnotes

Chapter 8

1. Lyle W. Dorsett, "C. S. Lewis: A Life, Eccentric Genius, Reluctant Prophet," *Christian History Institute Magazine, https://www. christianhistoryinstitute.org/magazine/article/c-s-lewis-a-profile/*.

Chapter 9

1. Thomas Cahill, *How the Irish Saved Civilization* (Anchor Books, 1995), 102.

2. Ibid., 116–119.

3. Ibid., 113–114.

Chapter 11

1. John Edwards, "Building a Virtual Wall to Protect Our Borders," *Electronic Design,* July 19, 2007, http://electronicdesign.com/ communications/building-virtual-wall-protect-our-borders.

2. Gene McConnell and Keith Campbell, "The Stages of Pornography Addiction," *Focus on the Family,* 1996, www.focusonthefamily.com/ marriage/divorce-and-infidelity/pornography-and-virtual-infidelity/ stages-of-porn-addiction.

3. Bryan, "The 5 Best Apps Available for Christian Men," Manturity. com, February 2, 2016, http://www.manturity.com/2016/02/02/ the-5-best-apps-available-for-christian-men/.

Chapter 13

1. Linda Nielsen, "How Dads Affect Their Daughters into Adulthood," *Family Studies, The Blog of the Institute of Family Studies,* June 3, 2014, http://family-studies.org/how-dads-affect-their-daughters-into-adulthood/.

Chapter 15

1.   Haka—Maori War Dances, *100% Pure New Zealand,* http://www.newzealand.com/int/feature/haka/.

2.   Melia Robinson, "Here's what is actually happening in a violent-looking wedding video that's gone viral," *Business Insider,* January 23, 2016, http://www.techinsider.io/maori-wedding-haka-dance-video-2016-1.

3.   http://www.folksong.org.nz/tika_tonu/.

4.   "Wedding Haka Moves New Zealand Maori Bride to Tears," *BBC News,* January 22, 2016, http://www.bbc.com/news/world-asia-35378875.

About Jeff Voth

Dr. Jeff Voth has a doctorate in leadership and spiritual formation, a master's in philosophy and apologetics, and a master's in divinity. He is a seminary professor, lead pastor at a church that focuses on community outreach, and the founder and president of CaveTime.org. Jeff reveals that most of his life's advanced learning has come from time in his cave, just as David's did—a place of refuge and safety, and a place to hear God's voice and gain courage for the battle. Jeff is marred to Lori, his wife of over thirty years, and they have four children, a daughter-in-law and son-in-law, and two grandchildren.

Author's Note

A portion of any profit made from *Defending the Feminine Heart* will go to The Pure Hope Foundation (www.purehopefoundation.com). Pure Hope is a ministry dedicated to strengthening families and restoring survivors of sex trafficking. It is an honor for me to lock shields with them as they do good battle in this arena.

A re you under assault? Do you need an escape — a place where everything you are, and everything you are not, is acceptable? *CaveTime* is *God's Plan for Man's Escape from Life's Assaults.*

❝ Regardless of who you are and what you've struggled with, report for duty and God can use you. How desperately the men in our culture need this book. Buy it. Soak it in. ❞

—CLIFF GRAHAM,
author of the *Lion of War* book series,
including: *Day of War; Covenant of War; Benaiah*

ESSENTIAL TRAINING FOR MEN OF GOD

THE SLING

5 STONES TO MAKE EVERY MAN A GIANT SLAYER

BY JEFF VOTH

Thousands of copies sold worldwide.
Available at CaveTime.org

The Sling is a companion piece to the best-selling men's book *CaveTime: God's Plan for Man's Escape from Life's Assaults* but is also a stand-alone piece to be used as a men's individual or small group study.

The Sling is not your typical men's book or study manual. Jeff gives you the stones, shows you how to use them, then the rest is up to you. Stand between life and death for your family, brothers, and all those you love. Like David, it is time to run toward your giants.

Slingers, are you with me?

VISIT CAVETIME.ORG
for your FREE gift

Words *From the Cave* is a one year devotional written by Jeff Voth. Each daily devotion is coupled with prayer and scripture to help give you framework for your spiritual journey.

BE A HERO

We want to offer you an opportunity to lock shields with us to reach the souls of men. We believe that *giving* is good battle against the enemy. Donating has nothing to do with money, but everything to do with the fruits that your financial contributions will help produce. Be a hero and donate today.

CAVETIME.ORG/DONATE

CAVETIME: A WORSHIP EXPERIENCE
MUSIC BY THE BRILLIANCE

Just like the psalmist David wrote about victories and defeats in his prayers to God— The Brilliance has crafted an album that helps you acknowledge the battle at hand, engage in fervent prayer, and worship your Creator.

CAVETIME PRESENTS
AN ORIGINAL DOCUMENTARY

Visit TheTrip.Film for updates

@thetripdocumentary

OUR MISSION: F.R.E.E. the captives

Fight Human Trafficking

Restoring Survivors

Empowering Advocates

Ending Demand

purehopefoundation.com
@purehopefoundation